THE THEATRE
OF GEORGE JEAN NATHAN

A Portrait Study by Arnold Schröder

THE THEATRE OF
GEORGE JEAN NATHAN

CHAPTERS AND DOCUMENTS TOWARD A
HISTORY OF THE NEW AMERICAN DRAMA

by Isaac Goldberg

AMS PRESS
NEW YORK

Reprinted with the permission of Simon & Schuster, Inc.
From the original edition of 1926
First AMS EDITION published 1968
Manufactured in the United States of America

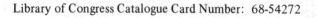

Library of Congress Catalogue Card Number: 68-54272

AMS PRESS, INC.
New York, N.Y. 10003

To
MARCET HALDEMAN-JULIUS

Preface

*T*HE *nucleus of this book first appeared as* George Jean Nathan: A Critical Study, *number 843 of the* Little Blue Book *series published by the Haldeman-Julius Company, of Girard, Kansas. That study, which has been subjected to generous revision, comprises Chapter III; the first two chapters are new.*

Of the documentary matter, the Introduction to The Eternal Mystery *and* Love: A Scientific Analysis *are printed for the first time. The letters from Eugene O'Neill to Mr. Nathan (excepting the last three, which have not previously been published) were originally made public in the columns of the* Boston Evening Transcript. *For that same newspaper (and, by special arrangement, at the same time for the* Morning Telegraph *of New York) I edited the Mencken and Nathan scenarios, as well as the prepared interview concerning their play,* Heliogabalus. *The Gordon Craig letters were first printed in the* Boston Evening Transcript; *a few minor passages have been omitted. The* Eternal Mystery, *which was printed originally in the* Smart Set *during its Mencken-Nathan days, has undergone some slight revisions.*

I am grateful to Mr. Eugene O'Neill and Mr. Gordon Craig for permission to reproduce correspondence that was never meant for print, and to Mr. Mencken for allowing

PREFACE

the publication of his embryonic plays. For the Index I am indebted to my wife.

As this book goes to press, news comes of the death of Arthur Bingham Walkley on October 8, 1926. The reader will kindly make the few necessary changes of tense in the text.

ISAAC GOLDBERG

ROXBURY, MASSACHUSETTS.

Contents

PART I

PERSONAL. BIOGRAPHICAL. CRITICAL

CONTENTS

PART II

DOCUMENTARY

Illustrations

THE THEATRE
OF GEORGE JEAN NATHAN

CHAPTER ONE

Outline of the History of a Man's Philosophical Knowledge from Early Youth to Old Age — 1. I am wrong. 2. I am right. 3. I am wrong. — G. J. N.

The Importance of Being Nathan

I

THERE is that smaller world which is the stage, and that larger stage which is the world. The critic of the drama, if he is to be anything more than a facile reporter of external impressions, lives simultaneously in both worlds, so writing of the lesser that it connotes the greater. The metaphor, of course, may hold true of all the arts and sciences, as of their critical practitioners. Who touches this book touches a man only because this man has touched life. Life in this sense, however, is as open to misconstruction as is " action " in the drama. Not all is " action " that is motion; not all is " life " that breathes and vegetates. Thoreau had journeyed far — in Concord, long before the birth of De Gourmont's globe-trotter, who remembered Rome as the place in which he had bought his red vest.

It is the peculiar quality of Mr. Nathan's dramatic criticism that it has maintained, from the earliest and crudest days, a close relationship to even the most pedes-

3

trian aspects of our daily living, yet without relaxing its grasp upon the deeper problems involved. It has been as obvious, even as coarse, as the man in the bar-room or the boudoir; it has been as learned, though never as soggy, as the academic in his sound-proof cubicle. Now it scuffs along on rubber heels that leave dark imprints on the shining parquetry; now it sprouts wings and, often to its own astonishment, cleaves the air. It squirms with contradictions; it kicks, it pricks, it glitters, it scratches, it leaps, it stumbles, it groans, chortles, wheezes, roars, sneers, spits, turns somersaults, evokes the jelly-quivers of the chemise dance, soars, sinks and comes up breathless for air. To the superficial it has only surface; to those with a touch of Nathan's own perverseness it has substance, too. Nathan's criticism is not only evaluation of the stage, appraisal of the drama; it is Nathan sardonically commenting on the great Tragi-Comedy, and — on himself. If he has made the stage live, he has made life theatrical. There are no critics in the history of our theatre, there are few in the history of the drama, who have so mixed themselves with their matter as to render a chemical separation all but impossible. In his writings the flesh becomes, — with all its weakness, its wiles, its imperishable visions, — the revealing word. The dramatic criticism of George Jean Nathan is not a temple; it is a mosaic, made up of fragments of his personality, often tesselated carelessly, in many places cracked when examined too closely. Yet when viewed at the proper distance it assumes a design and a meaning. It may well appear, once the numerous irrelevancies of journalism have been evaporated from his texts, that he has done for New York what Lessing did for Hamburg. Nathan, indeed, over a far longer period than the two years of Lessing's official connection with the theatre of that city, has written what amounts to a most unofficial, unacademic, indecorous *Manhattan Dramaturgie*.

We may get at the criticism through the man, as we may get at the man through the criticism. The one is as idiosyncratic as the other. In neither is there any essential concession to the crowd, unless it be the journalistic attractiveness of Nathan's paragraphs. Even here, however, I am convinced that this aspect of Nathan's style is appreciably deceptive; it lures the moth only to burn him. The man's disregard, not to say contempt, for the mob is so genuine as to be nonchalant. He simply does not care. His writing, like so much authorship, is largely in the nature of a public soliloquy. It is often irritating, meretriciously clever, it may even become insulting; it is certainly, for all its unseemly insinuation, for all its public scenery, aloof. It has an air, an aristocratic air; when his writing is most perfunctory, most careless, it yet retains the stamp of its origin, much as the prince in pauper's clothing. Nathan, in print or in person, is a character.

He is a character in both the psychological and the theatrical senses. Shrewdly, with a fine appreciation of what appeals to the popular fancy, he has fashioned an image of himself that is compounded of drama and disguise. In his most capricious moments he has himself become the puppet that he jerks about with unconscionable tugs, this way and that, until he reaches to something that hurts. For, who plays with the world plays at last with himself. From the moment he opened his show, Nathan the critic has stood concealed behind his marionette booth, deftly manipulating Nathan the character before the wide-eyed gaze of a public he courts and despises. What is it they have seen before the stage? And who is it that manages the performance?

The caricaturists of New York have missed, it seems to me, the opportunity to draw M. George Jean not as he recognizably is, so much as how from much of his writings he appears to be. They have not seen the puppet, nor its close, yet superficial, resemblance, to the puppet-master. They have not approached the remarkable " inductive synthesis " that McKee Barclay, in an inspired moment, made of H. L. Mencken, — a caricature that is in itself an excellent piece of criticism. They have missed the sneering sophisticate intent upon being displeased by everything; the immaculate parader, meticulously guarding his dress suit (imported, of course) from the pollution of cigar ash and *poudre de riz;* the bather in champagne — inner and external bath — dictating his article from within the folds of a silk bathrobe, swimming in waves of exotic incense. This is the kind of fellow that Nathan, producing a performance of Nathan, moves about the miniature boards of his marionette theatre; and there are moments when the puppet turns, takes his master tightly around the neck and gently, but firmly, changes place with him.

Nathan is both a sophisticate and a sneerer; he has not been afraid to take that step beyond the serious which

6

spells the frivolous. The twilight of his rooms almost symbolizes the indwelling sybarite. Not only is he a quintessentialized New Yorker; his destructive attitude toward the drama is but the sterner gesture of something that may soften into a caress, whereupon destructiveness becomes dedication. His quiet bachelor quarters at The Royalton, which Mr. Boyd has appropriately likened to a stage setting, are even more appropriately compared to the purlieus behind the scenes.

The man's whole existence, indeed, has been tinged with the playboy spirit. Long after he had been transformed from a local irritant into a New York institution, the aura of mystery and speculation surrounded him. His appearance, his habits, his pastimes, became subjects of amused or angered comment. He was bachelor, type *vie de Bohême*; he lived by himself in an eyrie overlooking the theatrical district of the metropolis, and his quarters were rumored to be furnished chiefly with drinking glasses and plays printed in impossible languages. He rarely went accompanied to the theatre; his extra seat was used for his hat and cane. Did a lady happen to occupy the seat beside him? The circumstance, at once bruited about, was almost equivalent to the flash of an engagement ring. There were times when Nathan left the play before the final curtain; in fact, more than once he was observed to stalk out before the end of the first act. Now and then an irate manager closed his showhouse to the caustic gentleman.

It was quite in the Shavian tradition. Had not Shaw, in the middle nineties, been set upon by the managers for his raucous laughter in the stalls? Had he not been asked to lower his mirth and — to dress more like a gentleman? Nathan, to be sure, opened no such loophole to the producers. He was — he remains — the Beau Brummel of his craft. Were not his coats always made with two breast-pockets, one for his handkerchiefs and the other for his horn-rimmed glasses? Was he not always too pictorial to be true? Had not that apocryphal biographer, Owen Hatteras, told us that he owned " thirty-eight overcoats of all sorts and description " — that " overcoats are a fad with him," — that " he has them from heavy Russian fur to flimsiest homespun," and even one with an alpine hood attachment?

The same Hatteras, in 1917, gave a short description that in the main holds true of today. Nathan " is a man of middle height, straight, slim, dark, with eyes like the middle of August, black hair which he brushes back *à la française,* and a rather sullen mouth. Fifteen minutes in the sun," avers Hatteras, " gives his complexion the shade of mahogany.; twenty minutes, the shade of Booker T. Washington." In proof of this I possess the only joint photograph of Mencken and Nathan ever taken, in which Nathan plainly looks like a graduate of Howard University. I may add that the sullenness of the mouth is promptly belied by the dancing eyes, which are perhaps the man's outstanding trait. Nathan talks as much with his eyes as with his mouth, which as often as not is occupied with a lighted cigar. The man has ease and charm, — the suavity and the nonchalance of one who has not worked hard for a living and who might not consider it

8

worth while working for too hard. There is, at times, a serpentine hint to his geniality; one feels that it could, under provocation, turn to bitter malice. At rarer moments one is even inclined to question its sincerity, for Nathan, undoubtedly, can "be nice when he wants to."

In religion, we are not surprised to learn from Major Hatteras, "he is a complete agnostic, and views all clergymen with a sardonic eye. He does not believe that the soul is immortal. What will happen after death he doesn't know and has never inquired." Nathan's *Eternal Mystery* deals with the illusory element in religion; he has confessed to me that he cannot approach, with critical impartiality, a play constructed about a biblical figure. If he is indifferent to the after-life, however, the here and now concern him all but excessively. His neuralgia, *via* the letters of James Gibbons Huneker, and of Eugene O'Neill, has entered into the literature of our nation. His hypochondriac affection for his symptoms was once the topic of a hilarious *conversazione* in the old *Smart Set* of unsanctified memory. Yet physical examinations reveal no organic defects, and he is still, at forty-four, eugenically fit.

On the social side, strangely enough, Nathan is defective. To him, a lie becomes a positive virtue when it may extricate him from a dinner engagement. A wedding is a nuisance, — almost a tabu. Callers, whether in the social or the business spheres, are intruders. They were not welcome at the *Smart Set*, from what we may gather in the account of Hatteras; they have been most cordially received, none the less, at the *Mercury*. It was once said that the telephone girl at his apartment had the names of five persons who alone would be granted admission to Nathan's chamber before five o'clock in the afternoon. Snobbery? Nervousness? Or self-protection? For Nathan, with all his sybaritism, is a serious if not a hard worker. Once an expert at outdoor sports, he has been for some ten years in retirement. He is at the *Mercury* offices every morning at nine, remaining there until noon, and at his desk in his apartment five or six hours daily, with a heap of finely sharpened lead-pencils ready for instant use before him.

A serious worker, yet always ready for a lark. The wit and the jester in him, the untamed boy, appear in the most unlooked-for places. Not only of his writings, but of his practical activities, he fondly makes a smiling commentary upon the life about him. A member of several metropolitan clubs, it never occurred to him to enter them until he helped in the inauguration of a club after his own heart. The *Club de France et d'Angleterre*, called "a supper rendezvous," was organized as a reaction against, a satire upon, the egregious etiquette of the usual night club. Its list of rules reads for all the world like the instructions to authors that used to wrinkle the brows of all prospective contributors to the *Smart Set*. It is, in very fact, a page of the quondam *Smart Set* come to life. The Club, proclaims its announcement,

Is the most exclusive supper club in the world. It is, in point of fact, so exclusive that it has no members. Its Board of Governors have blackballed everyone but themselves.

The object of the club is to establish a supper place in New

York where one may eat a Swiss cheese sandwich in peace and quiet. It has no other object.

The meetings will be held on Monday and Wednesday nights throughout the fashionable season. On each of these gala occasions, a select number of guests will be privileged the boon of sharing the charm and Old World atmosphere of the club. Each guest's credentials must be passed upon in advance by the Board of Governors. Under no circumstances will any gentleman be admitted who does not know thoroughly Anatole France, the waltzes of Johann Strauss and the Canoe Place Inn, nor any lady who orders breast of guinea hen and has not danced at least five times with the Prince of Wales.

All languages will be spoken.

Any guest who mentions mah jong, polo, the tango, vintage champagne, winter sports, new Paris restaurants or the latest mode in white evening waistcoats will be promptly kicked out. These topics are reserved for the waiters.

Top hats are obligatory.

A jazz band will be on hand to entertain such guests as do not know what to do to be interesting.

All guests planning to make speeches of more than fifteen minutes in length must submit same three days in advance to the Board of Governors.

The hat-check girl's name is Hortense.

It is requested that no one converse with the colored pianist while he is engaged in the performance of his duties. He is an artist who takes his work seriously.

No fist fights!

While the predominating air of the club is social and artistic, the windows will nevertheless be kept open.

It will be noted that the club is situated conveniently to the Third Avenue elevated and surface lines. Guests wishing to show ·off a bit may obtain twenty-cents-a-mile taxicabs in front of the saloon at the corner.

Male members of Europeon royal families sojourning in America will be privileged the use of the club rooms at any time. They may not, however, invite guests save under the provisions set forth in Rule 62, Clause B.

The swimming pool will be available from 3:30 a. m. to 5 a. m.

All complaints should be registered with the 31st Precinct Police Station, telephone Rhinelander 2900.

The club, in addition to being ultra-exclusive, is very snobbish. Its Board of Governors is stuck on itself.

Among the " board of governors " are Sinclair Lewis, Eugene O'Neill, Mencken, Cabell, Vincent Astor, Hermann Oelrichs, Condé Nast, Lord Mountbatten and Fédor Chaliapin. " Cabell," says Nathan, " is the most shrinking man I have ever met. He is, apparently, deathly afraid of meeting anyone and New York paralyzes him. I met him first about eight years ago when I was editing the *Smart Set*. He came into the office one morning and, though the day was a warm one, kept his overcoat on with the collar turned up during all the time we sat together. He is a taciturn fellow and, while suggesting an unmistakable self-confidence, yet deprecates himself in conversation."

" I'm not a bad woman," sobbed Mrs. Dane in her defense; and she was right. " I'm not a frivolous man," objected Nathan to me once in the semi-gloom of his rooms; he, too, was essentially right, as we shall have numerous occasons to observe. Yet the playboy air surrounds him, willy-nilly, even in his contacts with literary and critical personalities from abroad. Almost invariably they seem to look to America not for seriousness, but for carefree youth and a certain virginal vitality. Dunsany, Walpole, St. John Ervine, Walkley, Roda-Roda, Alfred Kerr, Reinhardt yield alike to the Follies.

When Dunsany first landed in this country, Mencken and Nathan invited him to lunch. He showed up in a fur overcoat of the paleozoic period, with only one button left on it. What would he have? Oysters. The then editors of the *Smart Set* ordered a dozen; Dunsany, however, interposed that he wanted three dozen. When they were forthcoming, the author of *The Gods of the Mountain* proceeded to sprinkle vinegar, ketchup, sugar and mint sauce. It may be guessed that the first impression made by the Irish stylist was anything but favorable. As he gulped the oysters, he began to tell of a short play that he wished to write for their magazine. Its title was to be *A Good Bargain*. Consuming the three dozen oysters he spun his fable, and before he had reached the end, he had, with its sheer beauty, paralyzed completely the suppressed snickers of his hosts. "After luncheon," relates Nathan, "I took him to see the Hopkins production of Gorki's *Night Refuge*. But after the first act, he confessed that such ' art ' was not for him and asked me to take him to a good American burlesque show."

So, too, when Reinhardt paid his first visit to the United States, in connection with *The Miracle*, Morris Gest, who had brought him over, met him at the steamer. Gest, eager to introduce Reinhardt to American art, desired to

13

initiate him with a production by father-in-law Belasco. It was about six in the evening, and Reinhardt, pleading a severe headache, said that he would be off to his hotel to bed. That night, however, Reinhardt sneaked off to see the Follies.

Reinhardt knew no English, and was therefore desirous of meeting some Americans who could speak German and enlighten him on American theatrical conditions. Accordingly Martin Beck, a friend of his, invited Mencken and Nathan to dine with them of an evening. They dined; but not a word was breathed about the theatre. The quartet spent the night — doing card tricks.

They order those things likewise in London. Nathan's first meeting with Arthur Bingham Walkley was at a luncheon at the Garrick Club, where Walkley had assembled a notable group of bibuli. Among them were Scott-Moncrieff, William Archer — the melancholy Archer whose delight, in his later years, was to read the detective magazines, — Judge Kellogg and a number of Oxford and Cambridge celebrities. In the middle of the luncheon Walkley suggested that Nathan tell the group something about the state of the drama in America. What would they like to hear about, asked Nathan, — the artistic productions, the new American dramatists, the ——? With one accord there was a yell of " No "! There was but one thing in the American theatre that aroused their interest: the Ziegfeld Follies.

To New York, to the Spirit of the metropolis in all nations as against the town and village, Nathan has paid characteristic tribute. The passage I am about to quote from *The Autobiography of an Attitude* may have been teased from Nathan's lead-pencil, as he avers, by a derogatory phrase in a review of a recent novel; I am inclined to believe that the apologia for Gotham was set down, too, with a live and antagonistic remembrance of Mencken's boosts for his home town, Baltimore, at the expense of the city without true homes.

In a review of a recently published novel, I find the phrase, " the artificial window-box life of New York." It is a phrase that, in one form or another, one constantly encounters in the writings of men who live in the hinterland or of others who, imported to New York, long still in their hearts for the great open cow-pastures. What is in the phrase? So far as I can make out, after prolonged conferences with myself, absolutely nothing.

The notion that life in New York is in the aggregate any more artificial than life in a small town is the not uncharacteristic reasoning of such persons as have been born to believe that human nature is forthright and honest in a farmhouse but is quickly perverted and corrupted if it takes a suite at the Ritz. That there is an artificial side to life in the metropolis, no one disputes. But this phase of life is confined very largely to more or less temporary visitors who are no more really New Yorkers than real New Yorkers are Parisians when they cut up in the Paris cafés and peep-shows. The New Yorker, by and large, leads a life that is no more artificial, when you come to look at it closely, than the life led by the average country-town lout. What is more, even the good-time-Charlie New Yorker, the flashier type of New Yorker, isn't at bottom much different from his country-jake cousin. He dresses better and he spends more money (because he makes more), but in other ways Julius

O'Grady and this lady's Colonel — jake and sophisticate — are birds of a feather. Both, to get to the main point at once, are ignoramuses. They have little education, little taste, little distinction — and not the slightest perception of refinement or beauty. Both are dolts. But their lives are cast upon much the same intrinsic plan, however varying the details. The rube lives in a frame house with the *châlet de nécessité* a block away; the New Yorker lives in an apartment with the *cabinet d'eaux* three feet from his bed. The New Yorker drinks genuine Holloway gin; the rube, home-made apple-jack. The New Yorker dances jazz to Paul Whiteman's jazz band; the rube dances the polka and the Virginia reel to the grocery boy's fiddle. The New Yorker negotiates his rendezvous on the Albany night boats or in Atlantic City; the rube negotiates his in his phaeton or in a hay-loft, and he negotiates them oftener, if the statistics do not deceive us, than the city man. The New Yorker, when he tires of his wife and can't stand her any longer, kicks her out and divorces her; the rube, when he tires of his and can't stand her any longer, goes on living with her and making the rest of his own and her life miserable.

And so it goes. If life in New York is artificial, life in Newtsville and Sauk Centre is equally so. If the New Yorker pivots his life on the making of money, what about the farmer? If the New Yorker, in the pursuit of money, cheats and swindles, what about the farmer? If the New Yorker does not go to church on Sunday, how much does the rube consider God on Monday, Tuesday, Wednesday, Thursday, Friday and Saturday? If the New York flapper bobs her hair, rolls her stockings, smokes cigarettes and is indiscreet, so to speak, in taxicabs, what about the country girl when the lights in the front parlor have been turned down and pa has swallowed his chewing tobacco and gone to bed? If the New Yorker sits up at night listening to a cabaret hussy sing " Who Makes the Dressmaker's Daughter When the Dressmaker's Making a Dress," what about the rube's sitting up at night to listen to the same flapdoodle over the radio? If the New Yorker thinks artificially, the rube doesn't think at all. When I read references to the artificiality of life in New York, indeed, I am reminded of the French peasant who walked two hundred miles to see Paris, who arrived at six o'clock in the morning, who saw a policeman patroling his beat in the chilly dawn and who, shaking his head sadly, observed, " Yes, yes, they are true. Alas, they are true, these stories of the dissipations and artificial life of Paris! What will happen to our army if its generals stay up all night and raise hell like that one there and don't go home until this time in the morning?"

2. *The Unimportance of Being Earnest*

All art, Mr. Nathan has said, is hedonism. To which it might be replied that art is, even more, mysticism, — mysticism shorn of deism and dogma. Mysticism itself, however, in this sense, as perhaps in even the narrowest theological sense, is a sublimated hedonism; the mind, as Bernard Shaw has lately discovered, has its orgasms as well as the flesh. Who shall say that there are no happy mystics? The king's jester, for all his tomfoolery, may be sadder than the monarch; he is also much wiser. Nathan is the devil's advocate; he raises hell. Nor should it, in this connection, be forgotten that the unchurchly phrase, though never associated with dignity, derives from the " mysteries " of the middle ages and referred to a scenic reality. Our critic has, from his earliest days, cast a dubious eye at mere sincerity in the arts. His very first book,

17

indeed, despite its often atrocious puns, its half-sober use of sesquipedalian words (" palaeocrystic," " bombilation," " metempirical," — one hears them roll off his tongue as they crack his lead pencils), — despite its cultivation of an attitude, is in some respects his most original. It is like no other book of dramatic critiques. It is natural to wonder whether, in that delightful array of *non sequiturs* which he has called *The Unimportance of Being Earnest*, he has himself been in earnest, been sincere, in denying the validity of sincereness.

" Your true artist," he maintained, " is seldom, if ever, sincere; for he realizes that to write only what he believes is to confess his pettiness, narrowness and inflexible limitations. Perfectly sincere men have been or are rarely artists. . . . The one way to accomplish things worth while is to be insincere, having a dexterous care only to conceal the insincerity lest the mob, in its ignorance as to real values whatever their name, be inclined to feel that it is being made game of. Where a man who is doing more for American journalism than Hearst — and where a more superb pitcher with the left hand? By the expedient of publishing unreliable newspapers, this gentleman is unselfishly encouraging the business of his rivals, and so building up what in, say, a few hundred years, will be a half-way honest and fearless national journalism.

" Where a man," he continues, with the same logic-on-a-holiday, " who has done more to make the mob appreciate the true beauty of the human form in the nude than Anthony Comstock — and where a man less sincere in

admitting the real purpose back of his nosings and sup-
pressions? " By these tokens Nathan has torn a leaf out
of the notebook of the man who suggested the title for
his article. One might carry the variations on the Wildean
title a step further, and indicate in Nathan the earnestness of being unimportant. He elaborates upon his
frivolity with a gusto that is in itself suspicious. He takes
his lightness seriously. And once in a while his essential
nature, breaking through the elaborate structure that he
has reared between it and the world, peers through the
protective screen of his levity. At these times there is a
deep, if muffled booming of an organ point that reverber-
ates beneath all the trills and arpeggi, all the leaps and
glissandi and forbidden intervals with which Nathan is so
fond of embroidering his scores. It is then that the heart
shines through the mentality. Such a moment was chronicled on one of the last Sundays of 1925, when Nathan, in
a nationally syndicated weekly article, looked back a lus-
trum and set down, in miniature, an *apologia pro critica
mea:*

> Just five years ago, in an article called " The Hooligan at the
> Gate," I delivered myself of the following observations:
> " More than any other force, more than any other ten forces
> all compact, have the moving pictures in the last half dozen years
> succeeded brilliantly in reducing further the taste, the sense and
> the general culture of the American nation. Like a thundering
> flood of bilge and scum, the flapdoodle of the films has swept
> over the country, carrying before it what seeds of perception were
> sprouting, however faintly, among our lesser peoples. And today
> the cinema, ranking the fourth industry in the Republic, proudly

19

views the havoc it has wrought and turns its eyes to new Belgiums.

" Controlled in the overwhelming main by the most ignorant social outcasts, by the spawn of push-cart immigration, by hereditary toothpick suckers, soup coloraturos and six-day sock wearers, controlled in the mass by men of a complete anaesthesia to everything fine and everything earnest and everything potentially dollarless, the moving pictures — the physic of the proletariat — have revealed themselves the most effective carriers of idiocy that the civilized world has known. Here in America, their fortress, they have cheapened a national taste, already cheap, to a point where cheapness can seem to go no farther. They have lurked near schoolhouses and seduced the impressionable minds of children. They have crawled up alleys and side-streets and for thirty pieces of copper have sold youth into aesthetic corruption. They have gagged the mouths of almost every newspaper in America with a rich advertising revenue; if there is a newspaper in the land that has the honor and the respectability to call the moving pictures by their right name, I haven't heard of it. They have bought literature and have converted it, by their own peculiar and esoteric magic, into rubbish. They have bought imaginative actors and converted them into face-makers and mechanical dolls. They have bought reputable authors and dramatists and have converted them into shamefaced hacks. They have elected for their editors and writers the most obscure and talentless failures of journalism and the tawdry periodicals. They have enlisted as their directors, with a few exceptions, an imposing array of ex-stage butlers and chauffeurs, assistant stage managers of turkey troupes, discharged pantaloons and the riff-raff of Broadway street corners. And presently they sweep their wet tongue across the American theatre.

" The moving picture organizations will — unless a miracle

intervenes — soon or late get a strangle hold on the native stage. Some months since, this hold was already showing its choking power. Now that grip is closing . . . one hears, faintly, the rattles. And save, as I say, a miracle stop it, there will shortly be not more than three or four freemen in the American theatre, not more than three or four men who will be able, or who will be permitted, to produce a play not designed for subsequent film use, not more than three or four men who will be the proud possessors of their own consciences, their own souls, and their own integrity. And to these men the present theatres will, save in isolated instances, be closed."

This article, together with the facts it disclosed, was greeted with a mirth Falstaffian in its proportions. I was set down as a blockhead, and worse; I was accused with the time-honored charge of attempting merely to attract attention to myself with a little extra-loud noise; it was broadly hinted that I must have been trying to sell something to the movie people without success. Not more than a few months ago, indeed, the Charles Frohman company, which is owned by the Famous Players, inspired one of its stars to publish an indignant interview in the *Herald-Tribune* ridiculing the facts I had been setting forth and attributing them to my incurable desire to stir up the animals for the sake of notoriety. And not a month in all the five years has passed that the body-and-soul-owned movie trade journals and the suspiciously susceptible and hand-trained movie writers for the daily press have not enthusiastically busied themselves in an attempt to deny what must now be perfectly evident even to a blind man.

The simple truth of the matter is that the moving picture morons have today got their dirty hands around the theatre's windpipe and that the theatre is beginning clearly to show the effect of it. The *New York World*, alone of our newspapers, has had the courage to look the facts squarely in the eye and, ad-

21

vising the movie advertisers to betake themselves to hell if they didn't like it, to set down those facts. But even the *World* has not told the whole story. That the Frohman company is backed and owned from eyebrows to toe-nails by the Famous Players company, every one knows. But fewer persons know that there are now five formerly independent producing managers who have signed away their souls to the movie companies and that, out of eight younger producers who have come upon the scene with independent productions since April 1, 1925, seven have been simply tools of motion picture companies. The papers are daily full of suave denials on the part of these gentlemen, but these denials are for the most part flubdub.

Another thing that the public does not know is that the current exorbitant theatre rentals — rentals so high that a newcomer or even a respectable old-time producer with a good play on his hands can't afford himself a hearing — are due very largely to the competition which the movie garbage-mongers offer to these producers. The movie blood-suckers are ready to offer absurdly high prices for theatres in which to show their slops and the legitimate producer must meet their figure if he would get a theatre for his decent drama. One can't entirely blame the theatre owners; they are business men, and a business man is entitled to get all he can get. And the movie people are waiting to give it to him if the dramatic producer can't afford it. All this talk about real estate values and the consequent necessity to raise rentals is bosh. The movie bidders have raised rentals and that's the long and short of it. And to argue that, if this is true, it is a peculiar thing that all the theatres aren't now occupied by moving pictures is to be so utterly lacking in humor that one doesn't appreciate that the theatre owners are simply at the old army game of holding the movie people's revolver in the faces of the legitimate producers and making them stand the gaff.

22

Fully half of the drivel presently on view on the New York stage has been inspired directly or indirectly by the movie people. It is either backed by them or its impresarios are backed by them; it is either pre-arranged screen material or the movie string tied to it is plainly secreted in its undershirt. There are star actresses whose movie contracts have to be filled out, while waiting, by movie-owned theatrical producers (names and dates on request); there are authors whose trash must be produced in order that the movie companies, under the terms of the contract, may get their better work (names and dates on request); there are contemptible plays that must be given a Broadway run in order to make them seem important to future picture theatre audiences (names and dates on request).

This, then, is the situation at the moment of writing. And, at the moment of writing, one thing seems clear. And this one thing — if I may make another prediction — is this: that, with the exception of a few producers of the stamp and character of Arthur Hopkins, there shortly will be in the New York theatre only the so-called independent small theatre groups who will be happily free of the movie influence and who will have to be relied on to stand by the decent theatrical traditions of the past. The Theatre Guild, the Greenwich Village triumvirate, the Stagers and the Actors' Theatre will, with the exceptions noted, find that the future of respectable drama in America will be entirely in their hands. To the right and left of them will spread the great movie sewers, weekly spewing out their potential film guano upon our stages. To the right and left of them will be a horde of producers clanking about in chains of movie gold and muzzling the press with enormous amounts of advertising. To them, and to the handful of honorable producers — men with something of the old integrity and pride in their hearts — will be entrusted what remains of the dignity of the American theatre.

23

And to them, further, the critics of the theatre will have to hold out a doubled consideration and sympathy. They will have need of it and they will deserve it. And the critics will be remiss in their duty if they do not accord it. For in the hands of the dramatic critics of America there rests now, as there never rested before, a weapon to save the theatre of their country and drive from it, before it is too late, the money-dripping, unschooled, grasping, foul and contemptible gang of moving picture interlopers. Ridicule and the ax, wielded liberally and indefatigably, will turn the trick. Let heads be smashed right and left, and let no mercy be shown. Let every one of these movie-backed dishes of tripe be stigmatized for exactly what it is. Let the critics have their Ku Klux Klan, too. That they will have it, indeed, that the white hoods are already on the way, my spies bring satisfactory reports. And I herewith have the honor to offer myself to the measurement tape for the first nightgown.

There is a little, as I have hinted, of the actor in Nathan, and he has frequently staged an excellent performance of himself for the delectation of his peculiar public. The world in falseface, as the title of one his books will have it. Here, however, we have one of the moments when the mask falls off, — when we catch sight of a particular cross under which he may enlist as a crusader against the crescent. Nor is the genuineness of his manner to be hidden wholly behind the frivolous garment of his metaphor. Here is earnestness; here is importance. Here is leadership in a cause. If I may put it so, there is a quizzical smile in the man's prose that is to be caught now and then on his face, half sneer, half amusement at the sneering. For Nathan, after all, is a serious person:

A Photograph by Underwood and Underwood

no Pagliaccio, weeping his heart out behind the stencilled smile of rouge and flour, but a fellow — as he himself somewhere has hinted — with the " mind of a gentleman and the emotions of a bum," whose chief preoccupation is his levity.

There are those, of course, who will never be convinced that wisdom may bubble from such undisciplined effervescence. Aristophanes must be dead two thousand years before ribaldry becomes classic. These the man is not interested in addressing. To the others, he exhibits his roistering criticism with a flippancy that sometimes disconcerts even while it diverts. What a language he has concocted to mirror almost perfectly his meaning! A trick mirror, indeed; for now it narrows and elongates his feelings seemingly out of semblance; now it fattens and shortens his thoughts and drags them out of focus to the very verge of unrecognizability.

I have connected Nathan's attitude with his lingo; I would establish between both of these and his chief service to the American theatre a connection equally vital. All three connote a remarkable power of what we may call desentimentalization, or, in curter parlance, debunking. It is more than significant that the solitary play that he has written by himself — *The Eternal Mystery* — should deal with an agnostic who, in the last moments before death, is converted through a cross accidentally made by sun and shadow. Here we have, paradoxically enough, the illusion of the theatre employed to criticize, to ridicule cynically, the illusions of life. Nathan holds no brief for the intellectual drama; the drama of sentiment he abominates; his peculiar problem is to find and foster the play whose brains and emotions he can respect because of the harmony that they have reached without self-surrender. It is here, I imagine, that the roots of his frivolity may be discovered. It is, for his peculiar personality, the wise course between academic solemnity on the one hand and, on the other, adolescent gush.

There is depth to this brilliance; there is melancholy at the heart of this lightsomeness; there is learning — much learning — at the core of this anti-academicism. To be sure, this rummaging through the *materia medica,* this parodying of the pedants, this toying with half a dozen languages, this eye-winking, this avalanche of tongue-in-the-cheek *non sequiturs,* this elaborate clowning, constitute the steps of a dance of wit that skirts many a danger, — a Witches' Sabbath of the spirit. To the virtues that Nathan has brought to our theatrical reviewing and dramatic criticism cling a number of cognate faults; they are the coin with which he pays for his qualities.

The unimportance — perhaps the uncomfortableness? — of being earnest. The earnestness — perhaps the compensation? — of being unimportant. The importance — the fun? — of being George Jean Nathan.

3. *The Attitude of an Autobiography*

It is amusingly symbolic that one may, without any substantial loss in the process, reverse the title of that one of Nathan's books in which he parts the curtains most widely upon himself. For *The Autobiography of an Attitude* reveals the fondness for topsy-turviness that has marked him from the first. In this attitudinous autobiography we find the prejudices from the angle of which he evaluates the world-as-spectacle and the spectacle-as-world. The gipsy of our critics — and gipsy is a favorite word of Nathan's — indulges here, without chastening, his whims, his fancies, his arrogances and his wit. Behind it, beneath it all is a raucous ribaldry that somehow manages to establish an equilibrium between alcohol and aristocracy, resting on the base of absurdity.

"Common sense," he proclaims, "in so far as it exists at all, is for the bourgeoisie. Nonsense is the privilege of the aristocracy. The worries of the world are for the common people. Meanwhile the elect may amuse and divert itself with tzigane philosophies" (again the gipsy motif) "and Puckish metaphysics. Only the cultivated, the well-to-do and the secure are safe and free to indulge themselves in holidays from acumen." It would not be Nathan if he did not subject this theme to a number of undignified variations. Prudent persons are supposed to save up for a rainy day; Nathan has a different notion of thrift.

Every man over the age of forty should put aside a certain amount of money each year for use as a nonsense fund. It is a rare man, and a liar, who will not confess to the possession of certain occasional idiotic sprees of fancy which he is unable to gratify. The regular and constant suppression of such wish-jags makes in time for a measure of unhappiness which, though funda-

27

mentally trivial, colors the man's days and life and philosophy. The wish-jags of every man need release, and this release they may find only through such a fund as I have indicated. The amount set aside for these annual sailor's debauches of the wish-complex-need not be large in the instance of the majority of men, for the majority of men's absurd wishes are in the main of a not very considerable bulk. They take some such form as a five dollar necktie or a dollar and a quarter cigar or a bottle of Charente brandy. But, though they are not great, a man's failure to realize them gets to him, as the phrase has it, and contrives to lodge a fly in the ointment of his mood. The man knows that he can afford to buy the things, but that is not the point. He does not buy them, or anything else of the kind upon which his foolish fancy has alighted, for the simple reason that they seem a bit too extravagant and unnecessary. A nonsense fund would take care of such things and make the average fellow happy. It would be a fund for him to squander with a grandiose nonchalance; it would not figure in his strict finances; it would be viewed by him in the light of found money or money won on a bet or inherited from a forgotten uncle. With it he might buy that case of Cliquot Ponsardin 1911, or that green vest, or that gilt piano upon which he has long rested a longing and frustrated eye.

Delightfully silly, of course; but was it Professor William James who advocated moral sprees? And hasn't Nathan, in yet another variation, struck upon a symptomatic index to man's culture? He is always skeptical, he has written, of a library that does not display a few grotesquely unintelligible volumes. " In the heart of every genuinely cultivated man there is a peculiar fondness for certain books that, though perhaps trashy and empty to some of us, are for one reason or another close to his secret fancy." And who says man's library says his heart.

The man's aristocracy quivers with strange overtones of democracy, even of emotional mobocracy, whether considered in the individual or in the nation. " Perfect democracy," he has averred, " is possible only, in a royal household," while England " is a democracy in perfect evening clothes." I have already alluded to his epigram that " the most delightful of companions is he who combines the mind of a gentleman with the emotions of a bum "; pair this with another — " Toward men, ever an aristocrat; toward women, ever a commoner — that way lies success." Relate it to a third and you have, in little, Nathan's vulgarity-in-aristocracy:

> In every thoroughly charming and effective person, one finds a suggestion and trace, however small, of the gutter. This trace of finished vulgarity is essential to a completely winning manner. The suavest and most highly polished man or woman becomes uninteresting save he or she possess it. In the soul of every fetching man, there is a streak of ingratiating commonness; in the heart of every alluring silken woman, there is a touch of calico.

Call this the rationalization of a personal trait, the attempt to make of an innate vice a virtue; it contains not only a quintessential truth but the explanation of much in Nathan that has at once repelled and attracted a host of his readers. Often he has been read with pleasure and then been condemned out of a sense of duty to the proprieties. Having himself flouted mere sincerity in art, he would doubtless endorse, by half, Mr. Congreve's

Witwoud: "a wit should be no more sincere, than a woman constant; one argues a decay of parts, as t'other of beauty." Yet there is a fundamental sincerity to his deceptive vulgarity. I say deceptive, because, to paraphrase upon one of his epigrams, his hooligan language has filtered his vulgarian emotions through the mind of a scholar. Somewhere he has written of the intense pleasure that a critic may receive from deplorable productions; surely, from this standpoint, his language is frequently the finest comment upon the merits of the work he is compelled to consider. To ignore mediocrity would deprive Nathan of a joy almost as great as that with which he welcomes genius. He tackles the fakirs and the incompetents with a sardonic gusto that has never been seen in the history of our theatre. Others have been masters of mere vilification, of condemnation that could not laugh and therefore grew moral. Think what it has been for Nathan to have brought laughter into our dramatic criticism. It is as if economics had been re-written in terms of the gay science.

Nathan is no Aristotle, no Dryden, no Lessing; he knows his little garden and he cultivates it. But that corner is like no other and the flowers he raises — queer hothouse Huysmanian hybrids they often are — have been liberally watered (sometimes alcoholed) with laughter. It is an uncensored, uncensorious laughter; laughter unapologetic, common at will, not from the narrow inhibition of the throat but from the tonic frankness of the midriff. "It is a critical custom in many quarters," he has written, "not to admit that what makes one laugh makes one laugh save the source of laughter be duly endorsed by the Epworth League, the American Legion, the Holy Church White List, the Ku Klux Klan and the New York *Herald-Tribune's* literary supplement. Being, however, constitutionally democratic in the matter of laughter, I usually and disconcertingly have to spoil the reputation for critical nicety that I have laboriously built up over so long a period by confessing that the saloon back-room species of humor not infrequently diverts me in a deplorably gross and welcome manner. I am, alas, the kind of ignoble fellow who laughs at Rabelais, a certain pamphlet of Mark Twain's, the unexpurgated Dean Swift, Walt Whitman's last words, General Grant's bedtime stories, and *Reigen.* I am, therefore, doomed to meet Abraham Lincoln in hell."

Laughter, to Nathan, is among other things a phase, a facet, of criticism. He has considered it, moreover, in critical moments that may be turned both for him and against, by which token he has endowed it with a breath of vitality. " Frivolity," we find him saying on one page, " is often the successful refuge of talents that are incapable of higher flights." And twenty pages later, when he has forgotten this flash of half-conscious confession, he launches into a serious defense of laughter that is characteristically compounded of " vulgar " reference, psychological penetration, sober reflection and gipsy rhythms:

It is not that the critic who writes lightly does not take his subject seriously; it is simply that, like a man with the woman he truly and deeply loves, his very seriousness makes him light-hearted, happy and gay. Beauty makes idiots sad as it makes wise men merry. Men laugh with the things and persons that are closest to their hearts. But because the rank and file of critics believe that there is something wrong with the kind of critic who, understanding thoroughly a thing that they themselves do not so thoroughly understand, takes that thing with a pleasantly careless whistle and the jaunty, sauntering swing of a cane, the latter is looked on with disfavor, and favor bestowed instead upon the kind of critic who would wear a long face at a ladies' day in a coon Turkish Bath. This is always the fate of a critic who knows his job so superlatively well that he can turn it inside out. The ideal critic of the multitude is not such a critic, but rather one who knows only half of his job and who conceals his lack of knowledge of the other half by taking seriously what he does not know, and writing of it even more seriously.

Confession and defense are both the man who wrote them.

4. The Blind Bow-Boy

At present writing, Nathan enjoys a bachelorhood that is distinguished by its consolations. Read him with only half an eye and you readily get a picture of the regulation leading man surrounded by an ogling chorus at the end of a musical comedy ensemble. He philosophizes upon his indifference to romantic, quasi-mystical love, which exists just as surely as he cannot feel it. Now and then, one is entitled to imagine, he does feel it, for a fleeting moment, only to see it vanish upon the wings of another epigram. He is content — and who shall say that he is too content? — to let beauty remain skin deep. At the age when normal boys write love poems saturated with drippings from Byronism, Nathan was composing a

32

horrific treatise on *Love: A Scientific Analysis.* In it he laid poor Cupid out on a dissecting table, in the operating-room of an insane asylum, and had at the defenseless bow-boy with a bistoury that curiously resembled the arrows from Cupid's quiver. *Love: A Scientific Analysis,* done at the age of sixteen, is the first long piece that Nathan essayed. It possesses a youthfulness that Nathan — both for good and for evil — has never outgrown.

For all its low burlesque, *Love* is important as fore-casting almost every form of farcical writing to which Nathan's peculiar temperament has lent itself. It is pon-derous with pseudo-scientific procedure; it is overladen with philological notes and self-conscious academic refer-ences; its " logic " is devastating; it exhibits, thus soon, the author's fondness for catalogues of conversation and his gift for catching life's platitudes on the wing. I won-der whether it has occurred to many that in this respect Nathan has done for the stage what Sinclair Lewis has accomplished for life in our towns and small cities. Nathan has transfixed the drama's flatulent repetitious-ness, its pompous commonplaces, its stencilled sapience. He has done this, moreover, with the one weapon that such complacency cannot withstand: laughter. His ration-alistic victories over love, which are as so many defeats, are accomplished with like strategy. When he lists the beliefs of the party-of-the-first-part to this amorous con-tract, he is already started upon the catalogue of imbecili-ties that is one day to become *The American Credo.* More interesting than these primitive indications of his later style, however, is the philosophical undercurrent of

33

the *jeu d'esprit*. The nonchalance, the essential coldness, the intellectual laughter at what his emotions cannot feel (this is an important aspect of Nathan's laughter), the inferential cruelty of the entire procedure, — these are qualities that are inherent in everything the man has done. At the age when adolescents passionately immerse themselves in the warm waters of illusion, Nathan is already standing dry-limbed and laughing on the beach of disenchantment. "Women," he has written, "as they grow older, rely more and more on cosmetics. Men, as they grow older, rely more and more on a sense of humor." In this respect, however, Nathan never seems to have been young. And yet, now and then as one clashes against his humor, one hears the clank of armor. And armor is more a protection than a weapon of attack.

Nathan, because he has expressed himself so freely about a function that is conversationally tabu may be easily mistaken for one in whom the element of sex plays an exaggerated part. He approaches sex with a biological freedom from sentimentality; he produces the uncanny effect of dallying in a boudoir which has as annex a laboratory. Yet, however deep the sexual foundations may sink, Nathan finds its rôle in ordinary life to be grossly exaggerated. Again, in the excerpt I am about to quote, I am inclined to find an element of more or less unconscious personal confession; Nathan criticizing the current view of sex is one part of Nathan criticizing, confiding to, the other.

[1] *Love: A Scientific Analysis* may be found, reproduced for the first time, on pages 253 to 262. It is presented as a juvenile curiosity to collectors of Nathaniana.

34

Sex, in the great majority of instances, is a much more casual and unimportant thing than it is customarily admitted to be. An idiotic conspiracy has sought, with almost uniform success, to make the world accept it as something of paramount consequence in the life of man, the ground of his happiness or unhappiness, of his triumph or defeat, of his joy or his affliction. Yet the reflective man has long known that it is nothing of the kind, that it is, as a matter of fact, of considerably less importance in his general scheme of life than, say, his tobacco or his *Schnapps*. Sex is, purely and simply, the diversion of man, a pastime for his leisure hours and, as such, on the same plane with his other pleasures. The civilized man knows little difference between his bottle of vintage champagne, his Corona Corona, his seat at the " Follies " and the gratification of his sex impulse. They all fall much under the same heading. He takes sex no whit more seriously than he takes, to put it superlatively, a symphony concert. He sees in it simply something always amusing and sometimes beautiful, and lets it go at that.

Well, the world itself grows more and more civilized as century chases century down the avenue of time and gradually it works itself up to the level of its more civilized inhabitants. And thus gradually the newer view of sex gains recruits. And what men believe, women in due time also believe. I do not say that such beliefs are commendable, for I am no judge, but merely an historian. I simply say that so long as men and women merely *felt* about sex, it was what it was yesterday. The moment they began instead to *think* about it, it dropped its mourning and wove vine leaves about its head — and painted its nose red.

In the course of man's contemplation of sex, one phenomenon has gradually impressed itself upon his consciousness above all others, and it is this one phenomenon that, more than anything else, has influenced him in his present attitude toward sex. That sex is a relatively trivial and inconsequential event in life, that it is of infinitely less permanent significance in his scheme of things than his work in the world, however humble the nature of that work, or his material welfare or his physical comfort or, as I have hinted, even certain other of his diversions, is clearly borne in upon him after a meditation of the history of sex life as it has directly concerned him.

One of the first things that strikes such a reflective man is the manner in which the brain cells themselves peculiarly operate to demote sex to a plane of unimportance. Such is the curious functioning of the male cerebral centres that the sex act, once it is so much as twenty-four hours past, quite passes from the memory or, at all events, from the direct consciousness. Although the fact, so far as I know, has never been articulated, it remains as an actuality that nothing is so quickly erased from masculine tablets of memory as the sex act accomplished. It is a mental idiosyncrasy, indeed, that the association of the act with a specific woman vanishes within an unbelievably short space of time, that so evanescent is the recollection that the woman actually seems a physical stranger to the man. What remains in the masculine mind is not the consciousness of the sex act, but only what may have proceeded from it, to wit, affection, companionship, friendship or spiritual, as opposed to physical, love. It is not an easy matter to set down delicately in type the almost incomprehensible degree to which this post-consciousness of sexual indulgence evaporates. Yet there is no man, if he will view himself honestly in the light of his experience, but will recall at once the peculiar sense of remoteness that has generally and quickly enveloped the woman with whom he has been on terms of physical intimacy. It would seem that nature, operating through the human mind, has contrived thus to make the world frequently a happier and more peaceful spot than it otherwise might be. In man's defective memory lies woman's symbol of chastity.

If sex were the important event in a man's life that some hold it to be, his mind would surely be influenced by it quite differently than it is. A woman, instead of so quickly and unintelligibly taking on the aspect of a complete physical stranger to him, would remain fixed in his sex consciousness. Sex would surely retain a vividness after its performance that it actually does not retain. Yet, such is the baffling drollery of human nature, that a man's wife ever seems to him a virgin.

Nathan here really speaks, not of sex so much as of the sex act. As usual, he is ready to forget a distinction if such forgetfulness will help him score a point. It is of *coitus*, not of *sexus*, not of *libido*, that his pungent remarks hold true. And even here, he has toyed with scandalous platitude. What has he really said, but that there is nothing like an excellent meal to ruin one's appetite? Does this therefore dethrone hunger? As little do Nathan's animadversions dethrone sex. *Omne animale post coitum triste.* Or, as Nathan would amend it, forgetful, philosophical, cynical. To this attitude toward sex may be related the personal qualities of Nathan's eccentricity, his surgical cruelty, his paradoxically gleeful indifferentism, his perversity that as often as not is disconcertingly pertinent.

In Nathan's philosophy, as in the application of his views to the criticism of the drama, sex is removed from the dark and dismal surroundings of the psychopaths and given its place, where it belongs, in the sun. It becomes, not a sin but an ecstasy; not a labyrinth of lures and aberrations, but a highroad open to wind and weather. It often wears, to be sure, a one-piece bathing suit in prefer-

37

ence to the hermaphroditic costumes that once blighted the seascape; it dances aphrodisiacally, as well it may; it can laugh, Hallelujah, it can laugh!

By the selfsame token, again, Mr. Nathan is uncensored and uncensorious. Live and let live; die and let die. His main weapon against the censors is the selfsame laughter that he employs against the pearls of mediocrity and against himself. Though he lays on lustily with bladder and slapstick, he recognizes that American literature and drama were never more free in expression and at the same time more free from interference than they have been in recent years. His objection to censorship is one of sound principle; it is the objection of the artist to the Puritan, — gentlemen whom in his epigrammatic manner, he has pertinently defined. " In a general way, it may be said that artist and censor differ in this wise: that the first is a decent mind in an indecent body and that the second is an indecent mind in a decent body." The artist, as Elie Faure has written, chooses to express, not to convince. Nathan, as critic of the drama — and, by implication, of life itself — adopts the attitude, the method of the artist. Much of his writing is to be best appreciated as a toying, an experimentation, with ideas. If, as a by-product of his irritating self-expression, he convinces others, that is their experience rather than his triumph. They can never be sure of him, however, and he is not at all concerned with being sure of himself. He writes, and having writ, moves on. He is inconsistent, illogical, impertinent, immoral, irreverent, irrelevant, — but the Comic Spirit smiled on him in his cradle, for it knew him as one of its own.

38

Laughter is often sadistic, and in Nathan the sadistic element is fairly elevated to the dignity of an aesthetic. Far beneath the surface of his personality, in some common root, his frivolity, his laughter, his destructive delight in criticism, his indifferentism, find a common nourishment. He revels, almost perversely, in self-exposure, and though he paints in his imperfections with tenderness, at least he paints them. If his enemies desire the backgrounds for an unflattering portrait, he has, hardly less than Freud, been generous with unsolicited suggestions. No doubt he has performed the service with something of the egotistic glee that Papini has felt in describing himself as the ugliest man in Italy. Self-denigration may be a form of self-caress, and whether we praise ourselves or blame, the psychologists are quick to tell us that we do but pleasure ourselves. Then Nathan's pleasure is double, and his written personal record fuller than that of any other practitioner of criticism in the country.

Nathan's aesthetic represents a strange balance between the real and the idealistic, the concrete and the abstract, the practical and the theoretical. It is no accident that he was the first to understand and to champion with equal success the peculiar qualities of a George M. Cohan and a Eugene O'Neill. Nor has he made his discoveries in a genuinely American art with the imposing self-consciousness of the native aesthetes. It is no accident, again, that he has proved to be our chief " de-bunker," our first detector of " hokum," or that he has performed these critical services with a most " uncritical " vocabulary. For much of Nathan's realistic approach is due to the element of cruelty in his personality. Nor is it the cruelty of the surgeon bent upon a mission that works ultimately to the healing of his patient; it is rather the largely objective interest — even the fascination — of the scientist in the laboratory, pursuing truth in its every detail, recking little whither it will lead him, needful to know what is, simply *because* it is. This is a cruelty inherent in all natural forces. It makes of Nathan a creature far less social than he appears to be, — a lonesome fellow, if the truth were known, forever running, like some Brutus of the mind, against the sword of that selfsame mind. There are Tenorios of the physical life; there are Tenorios, too, of the mental life. Nathan has decided elements of each, and each represents a path mile-stoned with dissatisfaction and disillusionment.

There is a passage in the Foreword of *The World in Falseface* that has outraged more than one of Nathan's friends. It is one of the central moments in Nathan's writing and concentrates into a single paragraph the personal aesthetic of the critic:

What interests me in life — and my years have . . . marched across the frontier of forty — is the surface of life: life's music and color, its charm and ease, its humor and its loveliness. The great problems of the world — social, political, economic and theological — do not concern me in the slightest. I care not who writes the laws of a country so long as I may listen to its songs. I can live every bit as happily under a King, or even a Kaiser, as under a President. One church is as good as another to me; I never enter one anyway, save only to delight in some particu-

larly beautiful stained-glass window, or in some fine specimen
of architecture, or in the whiskers of the Twelve Apostles. If
all the Armenians were to be killed tomorrow and if half the
Russians were to starve to death the day after, it would not matter to me in the least. What concerns me alone is myself, and
the interests of a few close friends. For all I care, the rest of
the world may go to hell at today's sunset. I was born in
America, and America is to me, at the time of writing, the most
comfortable country to live in — and also at the time of writing
the very pleasantest — in the world. This is why, at the time
of writing, I am here, and not in France, or in England, or elsewhere. But if England became more comfortable and more
pleasant than America tomorrow, I'd live in England. And if I
lived in England I should be no more interested in the important
problems of England than I am presently interested in the important problems of America. My sole interest lies in writing,
and I can write as well in one place as in another, whether it be
Barcelona, Spain, or Coon Rapids, Iowa. Give me a quiet room,
a pad of paper, eight or nine sharp lead pencils, a handful of thin,
mild cigars, and enough to eat and drink — all of which, by the
grace of God, are happily within my means — and I do not care
a tinker's dam whether Germany invades Belgium or Belgium
Germany, whether Ireland is free or not free, whether the Stock
Exchange is bombed or not bombed, or whether the nations of
the earth arm, disarm, or conclude to fight their wars by limiting
their armies to biting each other. . . . On that day during the
world war when the most critical battle was being fought, I sat
in my still, sunlit, cozy library composing a chapter on aesthetics
for a new book on the drama. And at five o'clock, my day's
work done, I shook and drank a half dozen excellent apéritifs.

There is an anecdote of Hegel writing through the
cannonade of the Battle of Jena, and asking at dinner

where all the noise had come from. One forgives Hegel; he was a philosopher absorbed in a system. He was, after all, oblivious rather than contemptuous. Nathan it is more difficult to forgive, — if we have been in the battle. And there may be a moral in the circumstance that the very chapter on which Nathan labored during that epochal day would in all likelihood never have been written had Hegel not lived. For Hegel, through Croce, through Spingarn, is part of Nathan's aesthetic ancestry. Elie Faure, in *The Dance Over Fire and Water*, has spoken of Montaigne as the " greatest of tragic poets in the modern world," — Montaigne, whom he pictures with " his back to the great wood fire, his feet on his footstool, in the depths of a forgotten plain, while outside the most terrible passions were agitating the most ruthless century. . . ." Montaigne and Hegel would have understood Nathan, without therefore approving him. We, too, may understand, without judging. For surely, if we transfer the discussion from the field of sociology to that of art — fields that not always are divided by the stone walls which critics build — we obtain a new perspective. It is cruel, as all perspectives are cruel. It is, to recall another book of Faure's, the perspective of the artist-historian surveying the career of Napoleon.

If, then, we are as surgically honest as was Nathan when he wrote these repellent lines, we must recognize — with humanitarian regret or with scientific objectivity, or with both — that he pricks us uncomfortably in a raw spot, by exposing the strain of Narcissus that runs through us all. He lacks the imagination to embrace humanity, but he lacks the intense selfishness that often taints obtrusive altruism. His very aloofness is a searching criticism of mankind. We may, indeed, regard him, from one standpoint, almost impersonally as an artistic entity.

CHAPTER TWO

Young Lochinvar Comes Out of the Middle West

I

GEORGE JEAN NATHAN was born at Fort Wayne, Indiana, at midnight, February 14, 1882. His father, Charles Narét Nathan, had been born in Alsace-Lorraine, the son of Jean-Jacques Nathan, of Parisian origin, and Renée Callot, of Thionville, Lorraine. His mother, Ella Nirdlinger, had been born in Fort Wayne, Indiana, and derived of parents who originated in Nördlingen, Germany, whence came the family name. Her father was Frederick Nirdlinger; her mother Hannah Mysorson. Nirdlinger, together with the Hanna and Hamilton families, was one of the first three settlers at Fort Wayne, which at the time was simply an Indian fort. Not a house had yet been built; but one broad wagon-trail had been broken. He had come thither with his wife, in a covered wagon, from Chambersburg, Pennsylvania, where they had first settled on coming to America. Nirdlinger was a cattleman and frontier trader who later did his share in building up Fort Wayne as a mid-Western trading-post.

44

First Photograph, 1882, and the Nathan Home in West Berry
Street, Fort Wayne, Indiana, in which Nathan was Born

Charles Narét Nathan was an owner of the Eugène Perét vineyards in France; he owned, too, one of the largest coffee plantations near Bahia, Brazil. Travel and learning, as well as business, were in his blood. He was a graduate of Heidelberg, one of the best fencers of his day, and a classic exponent of the Wanderlust. He lived, at different times, in almost every country of the habitable globe. Six years he spent in Buenos Aires; eight in Brazil, at Bahia and Rio; two in India; three in Pekin, China. His own father had been one of the leading criminal lawyers of Paris; his father's brother, Paul Duchelle Nathan, was professor of history at the University of Brussels.

Ella Nirdlinger, Nathan's mother, was educated as a young girl in the convent at Notre Dame, Indiana. As a child Nathan had often heard her speak of the quiet beauty and the devout manner of a certain schoolmate, Ella Quinlan, who came from Cleveland. Miss Quinlan afterward married James O'Neill; the playwright, Eugene O'Neill, who was later to be so closely associated in American dramatic history with George Jean Nathan, is her son.

We may discover at once, even from so cursory a glance at Nathan's ancestry, that he has been markedly influenced by the temperament and the activities of his forbears. In him those temperaments clash rather than harmonize, yet the strains are important and their effect clearly discernible. There is the element of the pioneer, which in Nathan has become metaphorical, aesthetic, perhaps due to the soft charm of his mother. There is his father's spirit of restless roving, which, though attenuated in the son, is sufficiently emphasized. Nathan, as we have already seen, loves the capitals of the world; he feels at home anywhere, so long as an air of metropolitan civilization buoys up that home. " To me, a nation is its metropolis. To that extent," he has told me, " as an American I am a New Yorker of New Yorkers. I do not like the country; I am a cockney. The country, as I see it, is for yokels and cows. In the city, life reaches its fullest flower. The rural districts are for arrested imaginations and city men when they get sick. I have not been back to Fort Wayne in twenty-five years and I'll probably never go back. Ditto, Cleveland. My future is in New York — and London, Paris and Rome."

In no very subtle manner the paternal ownership of the Perét vineyards may be linked with Nathan's dithyrambs to Father Bacchus and Lady Nicotine. Certainly the son's proficiency with the rapier and foils at college and later in American and European tournaments may be traced to the suggestion of his father's skill as a fencer. And it is not surprising that the son of a gentleman skilled in eight languages should confound his readers with references to dramatists out of the most recondite nations of the earth, and himself carry on the linguistic tradition.

When George Jean was six, the family moved to Cleveland. Here he was tutored privately and also attended school. From twelve to seventeen he received individual instruction in English literature and history, in French and Spanish. Spanish, indeed, was his father's

46

PHOTOGRAPHS TAKEN AT THE AGES OF
TWO AND THREE

favorite tongue; he spoke it fluently and wished his son
— "for what reason I do not know" — to master it.
Yet, though Nathan was moderately apt at languages, and
though Spanish is among the easier rather than the more
difficult idioms, it proved beyond his powers. Later, at
Cornell, he pursued it for two years more and then gave
it up as a bad job. German and French he had been
trained in as a child, along with his younger brother
Frederic. Their governess, Fräulein Laura Schmidtt,
who was with his family for years, was their tutor, and
is still alive, living in Dresden. Nathan's private tutor
in French and Spanish was a Pierre Decrain; in history
and English literature, Arthur William Harrold. For
Harrold, Nathan early conceived a critical aversion, together with intense doubts as to his educative abilities.
The youngster's private instruction included eight years
at the piano, under the tutelage of a "professor" re-
joicing in the name of Dr. Franz Beers. "A curious old
fellow who looked like an over-fed Hermann the Great.
His moustache alone was worth the price of the lessons." [1]

As a boy, Nathan was an omnivorous reader of history
and, indicative enough, of plays. After the usual youngster period of devotion to Henty, Alger, Optic, Captain
Charles King, Ellis and Fenimore Cooper, his youthful
tastes showed a sharp veering toward a more elevated
literature and we find him actually reading Goethe's
Faust at twelve, and, as he himself confesses, understanding everything in it save that which was important.

---

[1] Quotations from Nathan that are not otherwise credited are taken
from private letters to me, or from conversations.

At fifteen, he had read all of Shakespeare and, peculiarly enough at his father's orders, six of the Restoration comedies. As early as eleven, Nathan began to indulge himself in lead pencils and paper and produced " divers masterpieces of dramatic writing that were acted by the neighbor's children in a theatre, so to speak, which we had rigged up on the upper floor of the backyard family barn."

At the Cleveland High School the youth was subjected to the usual curriculum. He seems to have made a good record in everything but mathematics; algebra and geometry left him profoundly unmoved, and he was frankly bad in them.

It was in Cleveland that young Nathan first met the playwright, Charles H. Hoyt, who was a friend of Nathan *père* and had stopped over at the Nathan home on his way to Buffalo. Hoyt's *A Contented Woman* was due to open on the following Monday. " I was then a young boy. Hoyt had recently married Caroline Miskel and she was to have the leading rôle in his play. He told us that it was the most exciting promise of his life and that all the work he had done before faded completely from his interest in the light of this newest interest: the combination of his wife as his leading actress in his first attempt at what he considered to be a serious play. My father and I accompanied him to the opening. Hoyt talked of the drama very largely the way a good business man talks of his business. And yet he had a sounder love for the theatre than almost any other American I have since met."

48

Alternate summers were now being spent in Europe, chiefly between the months of April and September. In 1898 Nathan was taken to Paris, where he was under the instruction of M. Decrain. In 1900 he was in Italy, doing Bologna, Naples, Venice and Rome in a study of the graphic arts. In 1902 he was at Berlin and Heidelberg with his father, learning more German. During all this time, it should be remembered, he was an assiduous student of the drama and the stage. His interest in the theatre may be most directly traced to his uncle, Charles Frederic Nirdlinger, the well-known playwright of *Pompadour*, *The First Lady of the Land* and of the adaptation of Echegaray's *El gran Galeoto*, made popular by William Faversham as *The World and His Wife*. Nirdlinger, in fact, was to influence Nathan in more than one direction. It is he who brings the theatre into Nathan's life as an issue both theoretical and practical, since, besides being a playwright, Nirdlinger, among other things, served the *New York Herald*, the *Paris Herald*, *The Illustrated American* and *The Criterion* as dramatic critic. It is Nirdlinger, too, who is to suggest the journalistic career which the young man embraced after having been graduated from Cornell.

It had been planned to send George Jean to Harvard. Nirdlinger, who had done much to guide the young man's early career, was a graduate of that college. Nathan, however, had ideas of his own. " I never could bring myself to view Harvard as the right place for me; I did not like what it stood for; its English imitativeness was offensive to me. I chose Cornell for the simple

49

reason that it seemed to me, of all the Eastern American universities, to approach the German university most closely. I still believe that it does. Various eminent German scholars, incidentally, agree in this. In addition, it is a charming and beautiful place. . . . Another reason that influenced me was its traditional hold on Cleveland and the fact that most of the young men I liked and respected, my best friends, either had gone or were planning to go there."

At Cornell, Nathan took the so-called Arts course, specializing for the four years in literature, drama, history, languages and psychology, and obtaining the Bachelor's degree. He seems to have been as active socially as intellectually; he was an editor of the college daily, *The Sun*, as well as of the Cornell *Widow;* he was a member of the Fencing team; he belonged to the Kappa Sigma fraternity, was elected to the Senior Honorary Society, Quill and Dagger, was a member of the Savage Club, the Sunday Night Club and the Masque, served on various class and cotillion committees and drank his share in what he has called the various " bibbing vereins." He was chairman of the famous Cornell Spring Day, — the annual circus and jamboree of the university.

At college, where he won the Amsler Gold Medal for fencing, Nathan seems not to have neglected the cult of the body for that of the mind. In addition to fencing, he was expert at tennis and played the game for years. For five years after he left college, his devotion to the sport continued and he took part in various tournaments in the eastern part of America. Those were the days before gleeful rehearsals of symptoms, before a scorn for athletic perfection that would do credit to an ascetic, before pet ailments, recurrent neuralgias, and the general mortification of the flesh. Nathan studied fencing under Androux, the celebrated French foilsman, and Philip Brigandi, officer in the Italian cavalry. He had begun some three years before his matriculation at Cornell; he continued for some four years after graduation, fencing at different times in matches in France, Germany and Italy. Today his rapier thrusts have undergone a metaphorical transformation; the pen, literally, has become mightier than the sword. Nathan, four years past forty and not yet fat, has publicly abjured exercise. It is for men under thirty, he avers, and after that age does more harm than good.

Nathan had planned, on being graduated from Cornell in 1904, to take his master's degree at Oxford. His father's death in August of that year put an end to these hopes.

Considering the American university in retrospect, Nathan does not seem to have come away from it with any illusions as to its spiritual potency. It would be more precise to say that however much he may regard the universities, he harbors dark doubts as to the intellectual prowess — or even aims — of its typical student. It may easily be guessed, from an account of his own collegiate affiliations, that he knows the type of which he speaks, — that, indeed, he was at times one of them. His reminiscences, as suggested by a section of *The Autobiography of an Attitude,* are hardly those of the perpetual under-graduate.

The idea still persists in certain quarters that the larger eastern American universities are educational institutions, that is, places to which young men go in search of knowledge. Curiously enough, the idea is true. But its truth is not quite that which the majority of persons believe it to be. The larger eastern American universities *are* educational institutions and they are, too, places to which young men go in search of knowledge, but the education and knowledge that the average young man gets from them has infinitely less to do with Latin, Greek, epistemology, economics, the Purvamimansa system of Hindu philosophy and the Pali grammar of Kachchayana than with Irving Berlin's latest fox-trot, the right kind of pleated trousers, the way to make drinkable synthetic gin, the technic of what Scott Fitzgerald calls necking, athletic diversions, and the trick of going to New York for a day without the faculty's catching on to it. For one boy who is athirst for knowledge, who wishes to learn the difference between the theory of least squares and anthropogeography and what distinguishes the Battle of Echmühl from the Portuguese navigator Mascarenhas and the poetry of Swinburne, there are a dozen who care no more for knowledge of any shape, size or kind than a burnt-cork salesman cares for Dahomey. Ask twenty boys at one of these educational cabarets which they would rather know: the history of French literature or Ann Pennington's telephone number, and if nineteen do not answer the way I think they would, I am a very unobservant beagle.

There is, from the outset, an air of aloofness about Nathan. As a child he is reared according to an aristocratic plan; the effect of his private tutoring must have played an important rôle in at least two respects: that of a personal independence in judgment and that of an inner self-sufficiency which appears in the wayward aristocracy of his habits and his opinions. The high-school training may have done something to offset the influence of his early privacy. The fact remains, however, that today he is no " mixer," though he has a moderate fondness for social life that is distinctly prophesied by the nature of his college affiliations. It is important to remember that there is, in his personality, a blending of the Latin and the Teuton strains. Nathan's knowledge of the stage and its literature would do a German professor proud; his wit is flavored plentifully with Gallic salt; he has a shrewdness in practical activities that lives in strange but successful union with his sense of selfless dedication.

2. *Cold Type and Hot Youth*

Nathan's entrance into journalism was due, as I have observed, to the efforts of his uncle, Charles Frederic Nirdlinger. Previous to his editorship of Lorillard Spencer's *The Illustrated American,* Nirdlinger had been on the *New York Herald* as dramatic critic and as foreign correspondent. He had founded, too, with James Huneker, Vance Thompson, Percival Pollard and others, the famous *Criterion,* and was, moreover, a friend of James Gordon Bennett, owner of the *Herald.* Nathan, too, must have come well recommended to the late William C. Reick, managing director of the *Herald* in 1904. Reick had worked his way up from the position of a delivery boy on a grocery wagon in New Brunswick, New

53

Jersey. Later he had been helped, in return for favors, by Nathan's uncle, S. F. Nixon, who lived in Philadelphia, and by Nixon's partner, J. Fred Zimmerman. The net result of this combined family influence with the various powers of the *New York Herald* was a position for George Jean Nathan as cub reporter, at a salary of $15 per week.

A period as general reporter was followed by a series of special assignments, which included a number of important and conspicuous murder trials. Nathan was then transferred to such events as cup races and other sports, which he did well, even when he did not attend the functions. His fondness for hoaxes had already appeared. One of the Vanderbilt cup races, for example, he reported entirely from imagination. Actual details were handled by the sporting department; Nathan's contribution was the general atmosphere. On this occasion the night before the races — and a description of the night before was part of Nathan's duties — was bad, and promised a worse morning. Instead of discomforting himself in such weather, Nathan suavely remained in town. Long Island was speedily forgotten in the epicurean joys of a dinner at the Hofbräuhaus with James McIlhone, a *Herald* colleague who had the night off. After both had sampled a goodly flood of excellent beer, Nathan wrote a three-column story on the races that earned special commendation, and was listed on the bulletin board of the editorial room for its vividness.

It was on one of these assignments that Nathan first met James J. Corbett, — at a horse show on the Jersey

CORNELL UNIVERSITY FENCING TEAM, 1904

W. Bowman, H. Blount, W. Blount, F. Pino, Nathan, and Coach Androux

coast. The spirit of hoax lay strong upon the young reporter, and between him and the amiable pugilist they cooked up a magnificent story about Corbett's heroic rescue of a fair creature from the wild waves. Corbett is said to have been deeply affected when he read the account in the paper. At another time the imaginative reporter invented a tale of a mysterious hermit on Long Island. On the appearance of the story reporters from other newspapers were sent down to the scene, only to discover the fake. With a sense of humor to match their colleague's, they pushed the story along in their respective papers for the next two weeks. Nathan's superiors, it seems, were just as pleased with his fictions as with other men's facts. They liked his concoctions and never troubled to investigate them.

His next upward step was into the Sunday department of the *Herald;* it was, at the time, under the editorship of George Miner, later to be succeeded by Cleveland Moffatt. His duty now was to write two special stories a week, averaging between 3500 and 4000 words each, for which job he received $30 weekly, later raised to $35. In between, Nathan began, humbly enough, his career as a dramatic critic. The late Thomas White was dramatic editor at the time, and Nathan started as a third-string reviewer, being assigned to plays considered unimportant by the other men. The first play he reviewed was *Bedford's Hope,* a blood and thunder confection by Lincoln J. Carter, at the old Fourteenth Street Theatre.

Already Nathan was chafing under the cowardly policy of the paper. Bennett, of whom he has many anecdotes

55

to tell, exercised over his men an interference that easily and airily crossed the line dividing professional conduct from personal privilege. For all his show to the contrary, as Nathan recalls, Bennett always considered his big advertisers first and his readers second. It is not therefore surprising that the dramatic editor, White, should tremble at thought of the theatrical managers, should be forever apprehensive lest they complain about unfavorable reviews, should instruct his reviewers how to treat this production and that. "There was a minimum of honesty in dramatic reviewing on the *Herald* in those days. The theatrical syndicate controlled absolutely the dramatic policy of the paper."

Bennett, being himself a Catholic, would stand for nothing that in any way reflected on his coreligionists. Nathan was once sent out at midnight to cover the story of a man and woman who had been found asphyxiated in a bedroom on East 17th Street. It turned out that the man was a Catholic priest; he was lying with the woman stark naked. The *Herald* suppressed the true story, a peculiarly significant one in its various details, — and gave only a shrewdly colored version of the facts. The account is one of many that instilled in the youth a disgust for newspapers in general and for the *Herald* in particular.

Nathan was continually rubbing up against official bigotry, and rubbing it back. On one occasion, after he had been on the staff for two years, Leo Redding, the city editor, asked him to cover police news for several days until the regular man returned from his vacation. Nathan, in whom has never been absent a touch of uppishness, declined the assignment on the ground that his talents had progressed beyond such sub-arts. Redding, graciously accepting his attitude, replied: "Covering police stations is the greatest and most valuable experience a man can have in life." Upon which Nathan, with memories of police stations covered in his first days on the paper, and looking back at the situation after twenty years, makes characteristic comment. "This is one of the favorite schnitzels of buncombe with which newspaper men delude themselves."

What remains in Nathan's memory of the *Herald* era is a chain of associations and anecdotes rather than any lofty conception of journalism. In those days the favorite rendezvous of the newspaper fraternity was the barroom in the cellar of Weber and Fields' music hall, presided over by Joe Weber's brother, "Mock" Weber. Here, every night, a dozen or more of the gentry would foregather and sit around for hours. Another meeting place was Captain Churchill's restaurant, then at Broadway and 46th Street. There was Jack's, too, but the choice of journalistic patronage went to Weber and to Churchill. Churchill, as an ex-police captain, was on intimate terms with the newspaper coterie. Helen Green, — she of the admirable subterranean classics of Broadway life, — was for years a steady customer, often remaining till dawn. At Weber and Fields' café Marie Dressler was "queen of the revels in the dump and nightly came down after the show and sat around with the assembled bibuli. The late Diamond Jim Brady, Herbert Bayard Swope, Nicholas Biddle, and Foxhall Keene were steady customers and, upon their entrance, always drew a speech of welcome from the affable Mock, who looked like a miniature Ben Turpin or a caricature of Frank Harris."

It is to be feared that Nathan off the newspaper was as carefree, and as given to hoaxes, as he was during business hours. To these days belong his meetings at Sherry's, with Bob Collier, Finley Peter Dunne, John Fox, Jr., H. H. McClure, and other of their cronies in the literary and publishing world. Their custom was to serve peach Melba as the first course, whereupon — in accordance with an unwritten ritual — the peach Melbas would be seized and violently projected against the walls and ceiling of the upstairs room in which these hebdomadal festivities were held. On one of these occasions, it is related, Richard Harding Davis had been invited as special guest to meet some ladies of the theatre. During the evening Davis, who had been attracted by the charms of one of the young women, was overheard by Fox asking whether he might see the damsel home. At once Fox stole down, bribed a hansom cab driver to let him take his place on the box, donned the cabby's rubber hat and cape — and bided his time in the pelting downpour. Davis presently appeared, got into the cab and directed the driver to the lady's address on West Ninety-sixth Street. He did not get there that night. Fox drove the cab to Coney Island and abandoned it to the Island and the couple. Davis never forgave him. History, however, forgives, suspecting Bacchus and youth.

Authors in the early nineteen hundreds must have been

hard put to it for amusement, for there is an anecdote of another Davis, — Glenmore, commonly known as "Stuffy," who in those days acted as press-agent for the late Fred Thompson of Thompson and Dundy. Davis had been out one night with George Ade and Booth Tarkington, who were then inseparable comrades. One of their chief diversions while in New York was to hire a hack, drive up and down Eighth Avenue, and steal cante-loupes and watermelons from the stands in front of grocery-stores. On the single occasion on which Nathan had then met the two writers, they had just returned from such a cruise and were holding forth with about thirty of their purloined treasures at the bar of the Knickerbocker Hotel. The anecdote is illuminating; one hears it and understands the better such productions as *The College Widow* and *Seventeen*.

It was at approximately this time that Nathan first en-countered Huneker, whose favorite beer-chair was in the old Scheffel Hall, just off Union Square. "Here, nightly, Lord Jim would foregather with his cronies and by eleven o'clock the right arm of the *Ober* regularly be-came so weak that it was necessary for Huneker to make an elaborate show of massaging it, that the important business of the evening might not be interrupted. It was one of Huneker's boasts that he could tell exactly the brand of every known kind of beer merely by sticking his finger into a Seidel and touching it to his lips. If he ever failed at his boast, there is no record of it." The friend-ship thus inaugurated between Huneker and Nathan kept up until the former's death many years later. Their

59

THE THEATRE OF GEORGE JEAN NATHAN

meetings were frequent and Nathan has often said that, in all his wanderings around the earth, he has never encountered so dazzling and brilliant a conversationalist. After the beer at Scheffel Hall began to decline from its erstwhile proud standard, the meetings were transferred to Lüchow's and to the Hofbräuhaus. If, in George Ade's phrase, the cocktail follows the flag, Huneker invariably followed the beer. " Whither thou, Pilsner, goest, I shall go." A crony of Huneker's, as of Nirdlinger's, was Henri Dumay, a French wit and gentleman of letters who had served as editor of the *Criterion*. Dumay was regularly present at the early malt conferences and acted as an excellent " feeder " for Huneker's verbal pyrotechnics.

Later, Victor Herbert was to endanger Huneker's reputation. " He was," avers Nathan, " a gargantuan beer drinker. I sat with him at Delmonico's one night from seven o'clock until one and in that time he actually drank the restaurant dry of beer. We then repaired to a small drinking place next to the old Hofmann Brewery in the East Fifties, and Herbert, by actual count, downed eighteen more seidels in one hour. Herbert would travel twenty-four hours in a day coach to accept any invitation that promised some noble beer drinking. What is more, he frequently did so."

3. *Philandering with the Magazines*

Nathan's rupture with the *Herald* had been brewing for at least a half-year before he left the paper. The newspaper, as an institution, was intellectually subservient. Reick, the managing editor, "was an atheist so far as paying salaries was concerned and held them down to the Chinese coolie rate. The *Herald* thus became a mere shoddy business office, and, editorially, a joke. There were so many Don'ts editorially that it would have taken a vaudeville mind-reader to remember them in composing an article." Nathan had been approached by Lynn G. Wright, a former editor of the Cornell *Daily Sun*, of which Nathan, too, had been an editor. Wright was now editing the Knapp magazines, *Outing* and *Bohemian*, and suggested that Nathan run the dramatic departments of those periodicals. The offer was now accepted and Nathan set to work as dramatic critic and feature writer. His ascension to the new dignity he celebrated with a vinegary article on "James Gordon Bennett; the Monte Cristo of Modern Journalism"; he was definitely launched now as a writer for the magazines. He must have been definitely happier, too, in his new freedom, for Nathan never was by temperament or inclination a newspaper man. He had too much independence, impatience with routine, imagination, caprice in the presence of mere facts, — in a word, — was too much the artist by nature.

Now began a round of magazine associations. Clark Hobart, editor of the *Burr McIntosh Monthly*, which had been bought by Julian Ripley, invited him to contribute dramatic critiques to that magazine. The pages of Munsey's magazines were opened to him; though the name of Titherington was on the flagstaff as editor of

Munsey's, the actual editor, and the man who hired Nathan, was Robert H. Davis.

Munsey himself Nathan was not to meet until 1909. The Munsey magazine offices were then in the Flatiron Building and Munsey's own sanctum seemed to forecast the luxury of a movie by Cecil B. DeMille. " It was his practise," recalls Nathan, " to sit at a large desk on a platform raised three or four steps above the floor level, and when a man had an audience with him, to stand at the top of the steps and treat the fellow to a large dose of Napoleonic dignity. I had written an article for *Munsey's Magazine* on the Department of the Interior, some of the facts in which had interested Munsey. He called me in to discuss further facts before the article was put into type. Contrary to the general opinion of him, he was anything but a sourball. He was, indeed, a very amiable fellow."

In 1908 Nathan became associated with *Harper's Weekly,* edited ostensibly by George Harvey, but with the main work then being done almost entirely by George Buchanan Fife. The bulk of Nathan's work was on the theatre, and it was as a critic of the stage and the drama that he came at length — in the same year — to the notice of Norman Boyer, managing editor of the *Smart Set.*

The *Smart Set* period, both for the book reviews of Mencken and for the dramatic criticism of Nathan, forms an important decade in the history of our contemporary culture. I have already treated it from the standpoint of Mencken's development; [1] its significance in Nathan's

[1] See *The Man Mencken.*

62

career will presently be considered. Mencken had been engaged a month before Nathan as reviewer of books for the *Smart Set;* it was thus Norman Boyer who was indirectly responsible for an intellectual association that was to affect deeply the currents of subsequent American letters.

Nathan's critiques of play and playhouse became in the meantime also a great attraction to other editors. In 1909, Colonel Taylor, of the *Associated Sunday Magazines,* engaged him to write a weekly article on the theatre, to be varied now and then with other subjects. The arrangement continued for five years. In 1912 Nathan began the syndication to forty-seven American newspapers of a weekly letter on the drama and ran it for seven years. In 1915 he was called with James Huneker and Richard LeGallienne to the offices of *Puck.* Here the trio were offered a contract; Nathan was, of course, to do drama; LeGallienne was to do verse; Huneker, Steeplejack that he was, would preside over the other arts. The intention was to make of *Puck* the American *Simplicissimus.* For two and a half years Nathan dealt, not always puckishly, with the actors, playwrights and producers of his day and generation.

It was his attitude toward the theatrical Syndicate — a stout opposition, though his uncle, S. F. Nixon, was one of its leading members — that finally deposed Nathan from his berth on *Puck.* Nathan fought for a free field; he saw, clearly enough, that the Syndicate had done everything to bring order out of chaos in the American theatre,

63

— that it had brought decent conditions where before they did not exist. He believed, however, that if the art of the theatre were to be safeguarded, another type of producer must be recognized, aided and given untramelled opportunity. As a result of his campaign, Nathan was, of course, incurring those enmities which he dearly loves to court. A gentleman, by that token, more sadistic than sad. One of the differences inevitably came to a head, and it was through Erlanger that Nathan lost, from the list of his syndicatees, the Philadelphia *North American* and the Cleveland *Leader;* through Erlanger, too, who was a friend of *Puck's* owner, Nathan was relieved of his duties on that weekly magazine.

Always, however, there was the *Smart Set,* where Nathan reigned over the dramatic columns now with a scepter and now with a bludgeon. And if, on the sidelines, a *Puck* may die, there is a *Judge* soon to engage Nathan in his sempiternal capacity as judge, jury and hangman of the drama. For *Judge* he has served as critic, in his lighter mood, from 1922. Since January of that year he has been a consulting editor of *Arts & Decoration.* Last year he began, for the New York Sunday *Telegraph* and the Wheeler Syndicate, a weekly review of the drama, at a price that is regarded as the highest amount ever paid a critic in this country or elsewhere. Thus may the rewards of critical independence be chronicled in the language of the despised billboard. In addition to these American activities Nathan has recently begun to contribute editorials on American subjects to the London *Daily Mail,* as well as regular articles to the Lon-

64

don *Sunday Chronicle*. To the *Chronicle* Mencken contributes also.

Among the other magazines in which Nathan's name has figured prominently are the *Century*, the old *McClure's*, *Cosmopolitan*, *Hearst's International*, *Liberty*, the *Mask* (Italy), *Der Querschnitt*, *Die Literatur*, and *Die Neue Rundschau* (Germany), *Mercure de France* (France), *International Theatre* (Holland). A strange and motley assortment. But Nathan is not concerned with the place in which his articles appear. " One of the best pieces of advice I received in my *Herald* days," he has told me, " came from Finley Peter Dunne, creator of ' Mr. Dooley,' who was then on the staff of *Collier's*. ' Don't ever bother about the dignity or importance of the medium for which you write,' he said. ' It doesn't matter a damn where your stuff appears, so long as it is good. If it is good, the right people are sure to see it.' "

4. From Smart Set to American Mercury

People saw it. They saw it chiefly in the pages of the *Smart Set* as they see it today chiefly in the pages of the *American Mercury*.

The story of the intellectual and professional companionship between Nathan and Mencken I have already told in *The Man Mencken*. Much is there, too, about the *Smart Set* and the vicissitudes through which it finally emerged as The *American Mercury*. I am now enabled to weave a few new threads into the general pattern. For the rest, Nathan, after his first meeting with Mencken in the old *Smart Set* office at Fifth Avenue and Fortieth Street, in May of 1908, quickly became for the theatre and the drama what Mencken stood for in the other arts and sciences, — a banner raised on a goad, a general without an army and with no true cause, a fighter out of the sheer gleeful necessity of his internal secretions. Mencken, as Nathan recalls, " had come up from Baltimore to confer with Boyer, and I had been called over for a similar conference. Neither of us had yet started to do any writing for the magazine. We were introduced by Boyer. We left the office at about four o'clock in the afternoon, repaired to the Beaux Arts a block away and bought each other a Tavern cocktail, a brew made famous by that café. We discovered that we had many opinions and attitudes in common. That night we met again over the beer table and thus began the association of following years." Out of those common opinions and attitudes was born the *Smart Set* as it affected American letters from 1908 to 1923.

To the joint ventures, more or less cynical, which I have recounted in *The Man Mencken*, may be added a few.

Mencken and Nathan, sometime in 1916, long before *The American Tragedy* and Dreiser's entrance into the world of the movies and of fabulous sums for cinema rights, were almost responsible for a most original venture in which Dreiser was to be the chief figure. Dreiser was badly in need of money, and had spoken of his plight to the editors of the *Smart Set*. Mencken and Nathan, who were then acquainted with a power in the moving-picture business, procured for Dreiser an offer to appear *as himself* in a picture. Not only was the work dignified, since Dreiser was to be featured as " America's greatest novelist," but the weekly salary was considerable. Moreover, Dreiser was to act only in the introduction and the conclusion of the film; he was not to figure in the body of the tale. The project would have relieved him of his difficulties and won him a certain independence. Greatly to the surprise of the pair, when Mencken and Nathan went down to tell Dreiser all about it, the writer was grievously insulted. They were making fun of him, he believed, and still believes. By way of getting even with Nathan in particular, Dreiser bought and presented to him a complete set of Bertha M. Clay in paper binding.

Among the magazines of which Mencken and Nathan were advisory editors, when they were in partnership with Eltinge F. Warner, was a weekly started by Guy Empey, the war " hero," called *Uncle Sam*. Nathan and Mencken believed, at the time, that there might be some money in it if Empey could sufficiently work upon the patriotic sentiments of the *booboisie*. It was, incidentally, Empey's ambition to break into State politics. The magazine proved a rank failure; Empey footed the bills.

The other project was the inauguration of a Negro magazine, — one which would cultivate the arts and sciences, and not, like what was then the only first-rate magazine in the field, *The Crisis*, be devoted almost exclusively to politics. The venture had advanced well toward launching, but fell through. The conception, none the less, attests to the business sense as well as to the intellectual foresight of Messrs. Mencken and Nathan. It is since those days — 1919 — that the Negro has assumed a new importance in American cultural life; today we have a new appreciation of jazz, of negro spirituals, of "blues," of the Negro soul in general. The projected magazine, for all its hopes of advertising revenue from dealers in hair-straighteners, complexion bleaches, perfumes and other negro staples, was from its editorial standpoint to be a dignified organ. It would, undoubtedly, have played its rôle in coördinating the present renaissance of interest in things Negro.

Appreciably out of differences in attitude was born the *American Mercury.* Those differences, too, I have treated somewhat at length in *The Man Mencken.* They were beginning to be evident even toward the end of the *Smart Set* days. Nathan is interested in the arts alone; it is an intensely personal, even a selfish, interest, — aloof, aristocratic, antagonistic. When, after two years, *The American Mercury* automatically veered toward politics and considerations of a non-aesthetic nature, Nathan's active editorial interest in it began to wane. " I don't give a continental for such things," he says. " They are Mencken's fondest concern. The beauty of the world diverts me; the problems of the world are of utterly no interest to me. I have never voted; I shall never vote. I have never served on a jury. I never read political news. I never subscribe to any charity. An art gallery is more important to me than Vice-President Dawes. I have always been that way and I probably always shall be that way.

68

It is not a pose. It is the way I am made. I have no wish to better my fellow-men, save only in their appreciation of fine art and a civilized view of life. If a schoolteacher is kicked out for teaching yokels evolution or anti-evolution or anything else, it matters not in the least so far as I am concerned. (I believe in evolution, but what other such men believe, or teach, or do not teach, I don't care.) If Arkansas is an intellectual wilderness, let it be one. I shall never live there; why bother about it? I don't write for Arkansans."

There is not in Nathan, as there is in Mencken, an intense sociological curiosity that may sometimes be taken for a sort of inverted Americanism. In Nathan is not a trace of patriotism, explicit or inferential. His aesthetic outlook is allied to what I may call a negative internationalism, but an internationalism none the less. To the proletariat, which he disregards rather than antagonizes, he opposes a nonchalant *internationale* of salient personalities.

The influence of the *Smart Set* was a wide one and a deep. The inevitable opposition it stirred up was as music to the ears of its sponsors. Berton Braley, in his clever parody, *Three — Minus One*, symbolized the reaction of the intellectual bourgeoisie:

> There were three that sailed away one night
>   Far from the madding throng;
> And two of the three were always right
>   And every one else was wrong.

69

But they took another along, these two,
  To bear them company,
For he was the only One ever
  Why the other two should be;
And so they sailed away, these three —
      Mencken,
      Nathan
      And God.

And the two they talked of the aims of Art,
  Which they alone understood;
And they quite agreed from the very start
  That nothing was any good
Except some novels that Dreiser wrote
  And some plays from Germany.
When God objected — they rocked the boat
  And dropped him into the sea,
" For you have no critical facultee,"
      Said Mencken
      And Nathan
      To God.

The two came cheerfully sailing home
  Over the surging tide
And trod once more on their native loam,
  Wholly self-satisfied;
And the little group that calls them great
  Welcomed them fawningly.
Though why the rest of us tolerate
  This precious pair must be
Something nobody else can see
      But Mencken,
      Nathan
      And God!

The magazine, of course, thrived on such rhymes as these. They confirmed its power. It was emphasized a focus of intellectual rebelliousness, a rallying-ground for disaffected youth, a forum for the newer talents, a realm of discovery. Much that it printed, whether from editors or contributors, was of an inferior quality. But there is no other magazine that appeared during the years of its editorship by Mencken and Nathan that can show half its abiding effect upon the intellectual life of the nation. It projected new attitudes, it revealed new gifts, it campaigned for a free, virile, open-air joy in the arts. It had an honest aphrodisiac fillip that often verged upon vulgarity, but it was usually the coarseness of a finer nature, — Rabelais rather than the barber-shop. It chucked Minerva under the chin with a symbolic straw, and the learned lady, laughed. It freed the Muses from their chaperones.

The documents that were sent forth from the office were in themselves a satire upon the hollow dignity of the *Smart Set's* native confrères. Consider, as salient example, the leaflet, now rare, entitled

SUGGESTIONS TO OUR VISITORS

1. The editorial chambers are open daily, except Saturdays, Sundays and Bank Holidays, from 10:30 A.M. to 11:15 A.M.

2. Carriage calls at 11.15 A.M. precisely.

3. The editors sincerely trust that guests will abstain from offering fees or gratuities to their servants.

4. Visitors expecting telephone calls while in audience will

71

kindly notify the Portier before passing into the consulting rooms.

5. Dogs accompanying visitors must be left at the *garde-robe* in charge of the Portier.

6. Visitors are kindly requested to refrain from expectorating out of the windows.

7. The editors regret that it will be impossible for them, under any circumstances, to engage in conversations by telephone.

8. The Editors assume no responsibility for hats, overcoats, walking sticks or hand luggage not checked with the Portier.

9. Solicitors for illicit wine merchants are received only on Thursdays, from 12 o'clock noon until 4.30 P.M.

10. Interpreters speaking all modern Europeon languages are in daily attendance, and at the disposal of visitors, without fee.

11. Officers of the military and naval forces of the United States, in full uniform, will be received without presenting the usual letters of introduction.

12. The House Surgeon is forbidden to accept fees for the treatment of injuries received on the premises.

13. Smoking is permitted.

14. Visitors whose boots are not equipped with rubber heels are requested to avoid stepping from the rugs to the parquetry.

15. A woman Secretary is in attendance at all interviews between the Editors, or either of them, and lady authors. Hence it will be unnecessary for such visitors to provide themselves with either duennas or police whistles.

16. Choose your emergency exit when you come in; don't wait until the firemen arrive.

17. Visiting English authors are always welcome, but in view of the severe demands upon the time of the Editors, they are compelled to limit the number received to 50 head a week.

18. The objects of art on display in the editorial galleries are not for sale.

19. The Editors regret that they will be unable to receive visitors who present themselves in a visibly inebriated condition.

20. Cuspidors are provided for the convenience of our Southern and Western friends.

21. The Editors beg to make it known that they find it impossible to accept invitations to public dinners, memorial services or other functions at which speeches are made, or at which persons are present who ever make speeches elsewhere.

22. The Editors assume that visitors who have had the honor of interviews with them will not subsequently embarrass them in public places by pointing them out with walking sticks.

23. Photographs of the Editors are on sale at the Portier's desk.

24. Members of the hierarchy and other rev. clergy are received only on Thursdays from 12 o'clock noon to 4.30 P.M.

25. The Editors cannot undertake to acknowledge the receipt of flowers, cigars, autographed books, picture postcards, signed photographs, loving cups or other gratuities. All such objects are sent at once to the free wards of the public hospitals.

26. Positively no cheques cashed.

The external effects of the *Smart Set* style are the least of its contributions. Youngsters who didn't know the difference between Goethe and Gertie began to sprinkle their writings with German vocables; the college magazines often suggested vestibules to the offices of the *Smart Set* editors, imitating the " Americana " and " Rosemary " departments, the " Repétition Générale " [1] and those other

[1] The idea for the " Americana " that enlivened the pages of the *Smart Set* and were carried over into the pages of *The American Mercury*

73

Whitmanian catalogues of reminiscences, ladies, *conversazione* and what not. Everybody took to " fasting and prayer," addressed everybody else as Dr., Herr Professor, Reverend; every book became an *opus;* mediocrity was transformed into *pishposh*. Mere imitation, for the most part, and as successful on the whole as the legion of shufflers, young and old, who once tried to duplicate the inimitable feet of Charlie Chaplin. These sad young men have now grown up; they are on the newspapers as reviewers, in the theatres as producers and writers, on the magazines as editors. In their pages Mencken still meets himself, fasting and praying, spraying lyric vituperation over his antipathies; on their stages and in their play reviews Nathan discovers the youth of his spirit. Even the staid magazines of a former generation have put on new garments and rejuvenated their contents under an influence that is unmistakable; the hand may be the hand of Esau, but the voice is the voice of the *Smart-Set-American-Mercury*.

The *Smart Set*, however, was a dynamic influence as well. Here were discovered Eugene O'Neill and F. Scott Fitzgerald; here were introduced to the American public the plays and prose of Lord Dunsany, the poetry and plays of Theodore Dreiser, James Branch Cabell as a playwright; here were fostered James Joyce, Aldous Huxley, Thomas Beer, Ruth Suckow, Harvey Fergusson, Thyra Samter Winslow, Ben Hecht, John McClure,

came from a piece originally published in the first of these magazines. It was the work of Miles Levick. His article was entitled " Americana," though its content was dissimilar from the department as now known.

Muna Lee. The theatrical public read of names that looked like some frivolous inventions of George Jean Nathan: Molnar, Vajda, the Capeks, Lengyel, Biro, Heltai, Földes, — a complete Czecho-Hungarian invasion; Porto-Riche, Sacha Guitry; George Kaiser, Thaddeus Rittner, Friedrich Freska, Max Dreyer, Walter Hasenclever, Karl Schönherr; Giacosa, del Testa, Rovetta, Ferrari; Sierra and the Quinteros; Lennox Robinson, St. John Ervine, George Birmingham; Evreinoff. A patter song of nationalities.

Nathan's chief "discovery," of course, is Eugene Gladstone O'Neill.

The playwright had already published his first volume, *Thirst and Other Plays,* in 1914, through the firm of Richard Badger of Boston. His work had been produced by the pioneer Provincetown Players. Two of his plays, *Before Breakfast* and *Bound East For Cardiff* had been printed in the collection of *Provincetown Plays* edited by that tireless ambassador of the Little Theatre in print, Frank Shay. This was, to be sure, for O'Neill recognition but not yet reputation. The *Smart Set,* with its *enfants terribles* at the head, appealed to O'Neill as a likely vehicle in which he might be carried to a larger audience. Accordingly, as the playwright has related to Barrett H. Clark, " I sent three of my one-acters to the *Smart Set.* . . . They were all three 'fo'c'sle' plays, not at all the kind of thing the *Smart Set* prints. I wrote Mencken that I knew this, but that I merely wanted his opinion of them. I had a fine letter from him, saying that he liked them and was passing them on to George

75

Jean Nathan. I received a letter from Nathan also, and to my surprise the three plays were published in the *Smart Set!* That was my first ray of recognition." Clark goes on to say that O'Neill admits the need of modification in this statement. Not only had the Provincetown Players acted some of his plays, but the *Seven Arts Magazine* had printed his story, *Tomorrow,* and had accepted *In The Zone.* The *Smart Set,* however, "represented to him a wider and more general public, and recognition from Mencken and Nathan meant a sort of disinterested and impersonal critical approval." [1]

The three plays printed in the *Smart Set* were *The Long Voyage Home, Ile,* and *Moon of the Caribbees.* Nathan, voting the editorial Yes on the first of these, had sent O'Neill a letter to come and let himself be inspected. O'Neill came. Yet over so recent a meeting as this hangs already a deep haze. According to Nathan, they met in the old *Smart Set* "editorial chambers" in the Printing Crafts Building at 8th Avenue and 34th Street. "I found O'Neill to be an extremely shy fellow," recalls Nathan, "but one who nevertheless appeared to have a vast confidence in himself. We discussed his work for something like half or three quarters of an hour. He promised to keep in constant touch with me and let me see whatever he wrote. This he did." The first impression of Nathan, who has been O'Neill's harshest, as well as kindest, critic, tallies precisely with his latest. "O'Neill is a deep-running personality, — the most ambitious mind

[1] *Eugene O'Neill.* By Barrett H. Clark.

76

I have encountered among American dramatists, — an uncommon talent."

O'Neill himself, writing to me from Bermuda under date of June 14, 1926, tells a different story. " I can't for the life of me recall much about my first meeting with Nathan. It was with John D. Williams at some restaurant, I believe, and I was three-fourths ' blotto.' I remember thinking how much he looked like an old friend of mine who wrote animal stories at that era for Street and Smith. The second meeting was, if memory serves — mine is damned bad on such matters, let me add! — at the Royalton in his apartment, and I still have a letter written by Nathan a few days later in which he speaks of being gratified at discovering that I was as proficient at drinking cocktails as at concocting dramas. So you see. Suffice it that I found him warm and friendly and human where I half-expected an aloof and caustic intelligence completely enveloping and hiding the living being. *Half*-expected, — for his letters to me had given me an inkling. And a point to make is that we had corresponded — at rare intervals, it is true — for some years before we met, and I had sent him all my scripts for criticism as soon as the plays were written."

It was Nathan who persuaded John D. Williams to produce O'Neill's first long play, *Beyond The Horizon*, which definitely signalized the entrance of the new playwright on the American stage. The story goes that O'Neill brought the play to Nathan one morning, and that Nathan, reading it at once, had it in Williams' hands by six o'clock that evening. Before the next morning, the play had been accepted. Nathan then got Edgar Selwyn to read *Anna Christie;* Selwyn turned it down as "poor stuff," whereupon Nathan introduced it to Arthur Hopkins, with results already known. Behind the production of *Gold* by Williams, and the acceptance of *The Fountain* by Hopkins, were also the ministrations of Nathan. Hopkins, after a long delay, finally gave up his lien on *The Fountain. The Emperor Jones* would first have been published in the *Smart Set* had its length permitted. *All God's Chillun Got Wings* owes its immediate origin to Nathan's suggestion that O'Neill write something for the opening issue of the *American Mercury.* The play was delivered too late to be used in the first number, but it distinguished the second.[1]

Nathan, indeed, during the years that O'Neill was finding his place in the American theatre, served as O'Neill's first line of critical shock troops. He fought against a heavy opposition until the ranks of hostility were broken through. He has been no mere advocate; he has, on occasion, been the sternest critic of the man he discovered. The meeting of the two men was a fortunate conjunction; together they symbolize a new day for the American drama and the American stage.

It was one of Nathan's historical functions to open the windows of America to the winds of the modern European drama, and to effect a reform of American dramatic

[1] As this is written, Nathan has almost persuaded Gilbert Miller, of the Charles Frohman Company, to do *Marco Millions;* the decision rests upon Miller's ability to find a suitable, available actor for the leading rôle, a difficult one to fill.

criticism in harmony with the new sophistication. His career on the *Smart Set,* and on the various magazines for which he wrote during this earlier period, is coincident with the decline of Belasco as the ideal producer and the rise of the type represented by Arthur Hopkins and the Theatre Guild. Single-handedly he attacked the Charles Kleins, the Augustus Thomases, the George Broadhursts and undermined their prestige. Frohman was importing from London and Paris the stencilled product of those complacent capitals; Nathan ranged against them the array of his own Continentals. At the same time, Nathan was cultivating in this country the emergence of new American dramatic values. It is no accident, as I have said, that the man who " discovered " Eugene O'Neill should have been the first to claim for George M. Cohan and George Ade a talent that was in the early days dismissed as mere vulgarianism. For almost a decade, from 1907 to 1915, Nathan was engaged in virtually unaided combat against the academic, Puritanic attitude toward the stage as exemplified by the school of William Winter and Brander Matthews. His pioneer service in the " debunking " of the American drama he might have done ponderously, and with unimpeachable logic. He did it, as is his way, with an almost irresponsible gusto.

Today that labor, through the very success of its early efforts, has lost not a little of its primal pungency. Nathan must feel something very like to this, for he begins to roll his eye toward other provinces of our sad mortality. His stage becomes a revolving stage.

To the account of the founding of the *American Mercury*, as related in *The Man Mencken*, some minor details may be added. The choice of a name, as may be guessed from the long list of titles considered, was a source of much concern. The *Mercury* originated in the minds of its editors as the *Blue Weekly*. As soon as the project had run the fire of investigation and criticism, and had emerged as a prospective monthly, the name inevitably came up for renewed discussion. I append a fairly complete list of those that were discussed: *The Twentieth Century, The Capitol, The Defender, The Sovereign, The Regent, The Chancellor, The Portfolio, The Pendulum, The Other Man's Monthly, The Gray Monthly, The Colonnade, The Inter-Continental Review, The Athenaeum, The Colonial Review, The New Review, The Blue Review.* The name *American Mercury* was Nathan's suggestion, and it was Alfred Knopf's vote in favor that won Mencken reluctantly over. There was reason to believe that the magazine might be regarded as an imitation of the *London Mercury*, yet *Mercury* itself is a common name for magazines the world over. And as soon appeared, the *American Mercury* no more resembled the London magazine than the London *Mercury* resembles the *Mercure de France* or the *Mercurio Peruano*.

As the *American Mercury* now stands, Mencken edits it, with Nathan as contributing editor. Each owns an equal share of stock in it. Mencken, as in the *Smart Set*, writes the book reviews and, in addition, a monthly editorial. Nathan, as in the *Smart Set,* writes on the drama and, in addition, now writes the entire " Clinical Notes " department which is the former " Répétition Générale " (originally conducted by Nathan and Mencken jointly) in a more serious vein.

CHAPTER THREE

Don Juan
Oui, puisque tout n'est rien. . . .
Le Diable
Tâchons qu'un rien soit tout!

Première Partie, Scène IV,
La Dernière Nuit de Don Juan
— Edmond Rostand.

Zigeunerweise

I

THERE is, about the books of Nathan, a gipsy air of unpremeditation. Much that finds its way between these covers seems to feel that it does not belong there, like a chorus girl who has blundered into the British Museum. Nathan's books, like the poet, were born and not made. They grew out of the syndicated *feuilletons*, the weekly articles, the monthly reviews with which his early career was paved. They are, frankly, what professors call journalism, in the comforting illusion that books are alive in direct proportion to the thickness of the pages and the density of the thought.

The man, bibliographically, is slim-waisted. The first of his own books, as distinguished from collaboration, is

PORTRAIT STUDY BY ARNOLD SCHRÖDER

the stoutest; as if to atone for such early obesity, the second — *Bottoms Up,* 1917 — which followed *Another Book On The Theatre* by two years, is wasp-like in girth. After that an even balance is maintained. Nor is the balance only external. Nathan, at the outset, is more sentimental than he would have you know; there is a personal charm in his writing that he has begun only lately to recapture, by which token he has turned full circle. It would seem that the position on the *Smart Set* put him for an electric moment on his mettle. The very first book in which he takes his bow is *Europe After 8:15,* written in collaboration with Mencken and Willard Huntington Wright. It appears in 1914 and is altogether overlooked in the hurly-burly of a new war. That book, however — originally conceived as a series for the *Smart Set* — contains some of the best writing of its day, in which Messrs. Wright, Mencken and Nathan quite outdid themselves. There is a soft nostalgic note that now seems doubly of the past. The chapters by Nathan are those on Paris and Berlin, blended equally of a fond reminiscence and a disgust with the American perversion of both these quondam haunts.

Berlin and *Paris* are sentimental *scherzi,* the woodwinds playing a *legato perpetuo* against the persistent *pizzicatti* of the strings. At odd moments there is a brassy blare, a vulgar intrusion: but for a moment only, Nathan, at thirty-two, was young. His bias for Germany was a bias, not for pedantry but for mirth and song, even as his predilection for Paris rested on a love of laughter, not lechery. Wine, woman and song mean to him just what they say and not, as in the usual mistranslation of the Lutherian saying, swilling, prostitutes and drunken howling. His conception of art is tauntingly Luciferian.[1] If Art ennobles, it is by running usually counter to the accepted moral codes. The ennoblement lies precisely in one's self-assertion against the dogmas of the herd. Art's " greatest lovers and stoutest champions have ever been the men who most truly appreciated that behind its pretence of divine origin there curled a red and forked tail." Nathan denying to art the power of " spiritual exaltation " proves his point by wilfully transmuting that phrase into " psychic uplift." Yet it is because " psychic uplift " and " spiritual exaltation " are opposites, not identities, that Nathan may establish his main contention, — establish it, as is his delight, by paradox rather than by syllogism. They are right who, in their orthodoxy, fear art. For art, if not opposed to " God," is opposed to godliness. It is doubtless true that not all those things which make us " better " men and women make us better artists, and that not all those things which make us better artists make us " better " men and women.

The Nathan who, only yesterday, was protesting against the unexampled lewdness of recent productions in New York, is no moralist surely; but he *is* a gentleman of taste. He is the selfsame Nathan who, returned in 1914 from the capitals of France and Germany, was making protest against the debauchery of these cities by the American tourist on a holiday from his country and his

---

[1] See, in his latest book, *The House of Satan*, the opening essay.

84

moral code. "— But what is moonlight beside the fairy light in your eyes, fair Hulda? What is song beside the soft melody of your smile? Normandy is in the night air . . . '*man lacht, man lebt, man liebt und man küsst wo's küsse giebt.*'" Laughter, life, love, and kisses when they're to be had. It has its inconveniences, but it is not a bad philosophy.

Later he is telling his imaginary Hulda about New York, the " New York I come from . . . stunning by day in its New World strength and splendour, loathsome by night in its hot, illumined bawdry. Ah, city by the Hudson, forgetting Riverside Drive twinkling amid the long tiara of trees, forgetting the still of the lake and cool of the boulders that plead in Central Park, forgetting the superb majesty of Cathedral Heights and the mighty peace of the byways — forgetting these all for a Broadway! " It is, like so much conversation, like so much writing, a soliloquy. Nathan, from his days in 44th Street, from his nights in the Broadway emporia of plays, haranguing in reminiscence an imaginary fräulein on the bucolic retreats of Gotham.

At thirty-two, reminiscent and sentimental; next year, pert, at ease in Zion, self-assured. The material for the first of his own books, issued in 1915, at thirty-three, appeared originally during the preceding year; between *Europe After 8:15* and *Another Book on the Theatre* a subtle modification must have taken place. At any rate, it is here that the Nathan we know emerges, raucously, in high feather, clever, malicious, representing in American criticism a *frisson* decidedly *nouveau.* The book was

85

brought out by B. W. Huebsch, a publisher who has not, it seems to me, received sufficient credit for the pioneering he did in the early days of our literary intelligentsia; it was a venture, in those days, for a publisher to issue a book of dramatic criticism that was still inky, so to speak, in the columns of the periodicals.

Nathan, too, had the good fortune to receive a signal welcome. The book, dedicated to his then new friend, H. L. M., at once attracted the attention of James Huneker and Edward Gordon Craig. Huneker, on November 24, 1915, wrote to Mencken, among other things: " I read Nathan's last book . . . and enjoy him better between covers than in *Puck*. A writer more malicious, more brilliant and better informed unless on *our* beautiful drama would be hard to find. Paris is where that young man ought to be. There he would be appreciated. Here he only bruises his brain against the eternal box-office." Abroad, in Florence, Craig later anticipated Mr. A. B. Walkley's fondness for Nathan's so-called Americanisms in a short review (*The Mask*) that did not overlook the sense behind the style. " I think," he began in his rough-and-ready way, " this is the best book on the theatre that America has produced. First reason is that it is American . . . very American; it is good-tempered, rollicking, sufficiently paradoxical, well-written and alive. . . . The secondary value that the book has, that of being admirable sense, is thrown in as an extra: and very many people will want to know much more about the theatre, having enjoyed themselves in the society of a critic who can be profound without being dull."

When Nathan's *The Popular Theatre* appeared, Craig returned to the theme with a bass-drum *obligato*.. " It would be a mistake," he declared, again in his *Mask*, " to say that Mr. Nathan is as clever as Bernard Shaw . . . as a critic he is twice as clever . . . he sees. . . . Shaw tries to see. He feels. . . . Shaw thinks . . . that is the difference, and to us it seems so clever to be born with eyes with some sight in them. . . . To say that Mr. Nathan possesses a clearness of vision, a breadth of horizon and vigour of idea *seldom* found in present-day dramatic criticism would be to miss the target. . . . Change the word ' seldom ' to ' never,' and you hit the bull's eye. . . . Nathan knows. . . . I know . . . most people only half know. . . . Add to this that Nathan is an artist and let us all sleep the better for the fact." And, in 1919, Craig writes of Nathan, " the best of all theatre critics, to my mind."

Mr. Craig's hyperbole is a personal matter; it does not invalidate his criticism. As a matter of record, Craig and Nathan have never met. Their communication, which has been entirely by correspondence, began with a spontaneous letter from Craig. " I have never known a franker correspondent," says Nathan. " Accused of fraud and pretence, he is as completely honest a man as I have ever known. He is, to my mind, the one wholly, sincere man in the world of the modern theatre." On three occasions Nathan has started from London or Paris for Rapallo, Italy, to meet Craig, and each time something has intervened. Once Nathan fell ill in Paris. Another time he had to hurry back to the United States to discuss the sale of the *Smart Set* to Hearst and the founding of the *American Mercury*. As appears from a perusal of the letters from Craig to Nathan, the American has been untiring in his efforts to interest domestic producers in the importation of the Italianate Englishman. It looked, for a time, as if Hopkins, who has a genuine appreciation of Craig, would raise the money to bring him over. With the exception of Morris Gest, no other impresario looms as a possibility.

The other books of Nathan require no special comment here; they will presently be treated as a body of criticism. There is little about their growth that is organic, yet they are the product of a keen, if erratic, mind that lends to them a true unity of conception.

Of *Heliogabalus* there is this to add to what I have said of it in *The Man Mencken*. The authors, I believe, were disappointed in its failure to rouse the virtuous rabble. They had evidently looked for a *succès de scandale*; they were prepared, indeed, despite its appearance in a private edition, for an intellectual raid of the " smuthounds." Here, in fact, was a super-bedroom-farce that adds to moral insult religious injury, — " a hell-broth of wit, humor, fantasy and downright idol-smashing," as Steeplejack Huneker had written in the New York *World*, " one of the most brilliant farces I've read since Gilbert's or Shaw's." Public opposition, however, was not forthcoming; more's the pity, since the collaborators had prepared a statement bristling with the righteous indignation of outraged authorship. I transcribe it from the typewritten sheets originally prepared for the press; even today it

88

reads lively enough to merit the resurrection of print. More: it contains a kernel of truth that lifts it above the puddles of your average, inept press agentry. Reading it even at this late date one conjures up not without a smile a mental image of the caustic collaborators standing before the assembled newspaper men, defending themselves against their own attack. It is affecting. Also, it is theatrical. It is, in its way, Heliogabalian. One with an impersonal, largely aesthetic attitude toward life can only regret that *Heliogabalus* wasn't pounced upon by those whom Nathan elegantly calls the "smut-smellers." What a charming side-show we missed!

It is a Gilbertian moment, and yet — and yet, it is none the less a serious document. For *Heliogabalus* is a play that should be known. Whatever its faults, it may yet prove to be the best bedroom farce ever written in these United States — one, indeed, with a moral, though it be a Roman moral rather than a Christian. You are to imagine, then, a public scandal over the play. Enter the authors, surrounded by a bevy of bobbed-hair ladies of the press.

These proceedings are typically simian. For four or five years past the stages of Broadway have been chiefly occupied by bedroom farces of an almost incredible indecency. Now, venturing to have at these inane obscenities with satire, we find ourselves attacked by the very Puritans who permitted the original works to go unchallenged. In other words, we discover that it is perfectly safe in New York to be grossly indecent, but that it is dangerous to heave a cobblestone at indecency.

Heliogabalus is not offered for production in America. We

have no desire to put it into commercial competition with such plays as it attacks. Our European agents, however, have arranged for its early presentation in three of the countries of the Continent, and negotiations are under way for its performance in two others. It will be played by first-rate actors and under the supervision of directors of international reputation.

As a printed play it is not and never has been offered to the general public. It was published in a limited and expensive edition for the civilized minority only, and that edition was sold out in advance of publication. Thus its prohibition at the present moment, either as a book or as an acting play, can serve no intelligible end. In point of fact, no intelligible end is aimed at. The one purpose of organized Comstockery is to squeeze money out of pious blockheads by giving them a good show.

In this case the show will undoubtedly be good; in fact, we make that specific promise to the nobility and gentry. But it will not be the usual one-sided lynching. On the contrary, we shall take the offensive ourselves, and push both the original complainant and our claim for damages to decision in the highest courts. We are prepared to prove that the whole proceedings are disingenuous and malicious, and we shall not spare time, energy or money until every organization concerned has paid heavily for its fun, and every individual has been taught, once and for all time, that the machinery of the law cannot be safely debased to private and nefarious uses.

Heliogabalus, as any one may discover by the simple device of reading it, is absolutely clean. If persons of filthy imagination read obscene meanings into it, then the fault is surely not ours. Nor will it be our fault if they come out of this case, as we confidently expect and predict, wishing heartily that they had kept their erotic fancy in better check."

Are not these the very accents of injured authorship rising to the defense of intellectual freedom? Overtones of the Areopagitica! A thousand pities that after such a splendid dress rehearsal the curtain never rose on the comedy of " The People *vs.* Heliogabalus." [1]

The single venture of Nathan into the writing of plays, as distinguished from his collaboration with Mencken in *Heliogabalus,* had a short but lively career. *The Eternal Mystery* is a one-acter; it appears now in final revision, together with the hitherto unprinted Introduction originally devised for its publication in 1918. The play itself dates back to 1913, when it was produced before a single audience at the Princess Theatre, New York. The managers of the theatre, by a vote of three to one, ordered its immediate suppression on the ground that it was sacrilegious. Yet when, soon after, the play was given in the Little Theatre of Philadelphia and the Pitt Theatre, Pittsburgh, it injured the susceptibilities of none, and had a prosperous run. Encouraged by this, Mr. William Moore Patch, director of the Pitt, took the play to the Washington Theatre, Detroit. But lo, the directors of the theatre, after a single performance, ordained its with-

---

[1] That this pronunciamento was more than journalistic pretense was proved by Mencken's prompt action in the case of the attempted suppression of *The American Mercury* for April, 1926, by J. Frank Chase, head of the Massachusetts *Watch and Ward Society.* Nathan is not interested in the practical details of free speech. Mencken, however, rushed to Boston, had himself arrested for selling a copy of the proscribed publication to the Reverend Mr. Chase himself, and to the surprise of everybody — including Mr. Mencken — won a complete victory. At the time of writing a countersuit for damages, filed by Mencken against Chase and his society, is pending.

drawal. The piece was impious. Just as William A. Brady had done in New York, so Mr. Patch resigned, in protest, from the management of the theatre. As a result of these adventures, Nathan decided to withdraw the play from American production, making the one exception of the city of Chicago, — " a rational and evenly balanced community."

The Foreword to the play [1] is not without characteristic gaps in the Nathanian logic. To take the last first, when a good critic writes a bad play he may remain a good critic, but he is none the less a bad playwright. And if I take money for making a bad table, I may hardly offer in extenuation the alleged truth that I am an excellent chef. People want to use my table, not eat it. Not that *The Eternal Mystery* is a bad play, though it is a long distance from being a fine one. Similarly, there is something specious in Nathan's apologia as to irreverence. Here is a short thesis of life as a great illusion, with religion as one of the component illusions. And the thesis is driven home by a *tour de force* of stage hokum.

It is easy to see, even from a reading, that it would affect its audiences tremendously — in either a favorable or an unfavorable manner — for reasons definitely removed from dramatic aesthetics. As a piece of dramaturgy it is certainly obvious and economical enough, except for the exegetical tirade of the dying man, who becomes as long-winded as an Italian prima donna in the throes of her last aria, expiring of tuberculosis at the weight of 190 pounds. Essentially — and here Nathan's

[1] See page 231.

apologia holds true — it is no more sacrilegious than is any philosophy of illusion. Had it employed as the background of its thesis any theme other than religion, it would surely not have aroused in some quarters the opposition with which it met. A play might easily be written by some minister or rabbi or priest with technical ability in the drama, revealing the illusion that nourishes the so-called men of science, or of art. Aesthetically considered, the play deals by implication with any and all illusions, and with the desire of man to erect as his truth the pleasantest lie. Fundamentally, then, *The Eternal Mystery* is not anti-religious so much as it is a cynical presentation of man's boasted rationalism. Is there not here — if we are seeking cause for offense — just as much reason for the hostility of the rationalists? Is Jim a pleasant spectacle in the eyes of those whose shelves are freighted with Huxley and Darwin and Nietzsche — and Nathan? By this token Nathan has written a little piece that bites below the surface and cuts both ways.

The mystery remains. To see in the piece only a dramatized cracker-box atheism is to miss its central cynicism. As always, Nathan as critic practices his criticism upon himself no less than upon others.

2. *The World As Drama*

There is a literal sense in which, to Nathan, all the world's a stage, and he the critic of the performance. A row of footlights intervenes between the actors on that vast stage and Mr. Nathan, seated in his coign of vantage, chary of applause, yet not niggardly with it. So ready he is to make mock of the human puppets that one suspects some deeply underlying moments of melancholy. At times he splits in two; he becomes both actor and critic, and makes merriest mock of himself. For Nathan's theatrical and dramatic criticism is avowedly autobiography in terms of critical comment. It is difficult to speak of his philosophic foundations; foundations connote broad, solid bases. The foundations of Nathan's anti-philosophy suggest rather the balancing of a pyramid on its apex; everything is there — solidity, shape, size — everything but that deceptive stability with which philosophers laboriously endow their systems, only to have them collapse not so much from top- as from bottom-heaviness. Nathan conceives the world in terms of doubt. The very first words of his *Materia Critica* proclaim an *ars critica* that might have been deduced from any of the half-dozen volumes that preceded it, — an *ars critica* which is, for him, likewise an *ars vivendi*. Once and for all he has shorn it of all pedagogical trimmings and restored it to its major function as highly personalized artistry:

As a critic, it has never been my aim or purpose to convince anyone, including myself. My sole effort has been to express personal opinions grounded upon such training and experience and the philosophy deduced therefrom as I may possess. Since I personally am not fool enough to believe finally in everything that I happen at the moment to believe, however stoutly, I am not fool enough to wish to convince anyone finally in matters that, at their very best, are in all probability of a dubious truth. I please myself to believe that the critic who has another aim is

a vainglorious and often absurd figure. One is a good critic in
the degree that one is able to answer vacillating and quibbling
doubt with determined and persuasively positive doubt. Criticism
is the prevailing of intelligent skepticism over vague and be-
fuddled prejudice and uncertainty. It answers no riddle; it
merely poses an oppugnant and contradictory riddle. When the
critic ceases to have self-doubts, he ceases to be a critic and becomes a pedagogue.

Allied to this fundamental dubiety is Mr. Nathan's
noticeable mistrust of the emotions. A psychologist might
contend that the shifting sands upon which such a philosophic attitude is built were themselves the best proof of its
emotional origin. Nathan himself is aware, without any
Freudian fireworks, that art — and therefore criticism,
and therefore, more than is suspected, science — derives
largely from the unconscious, and that it is difficult, if not
downright impossible, to track the genetic impulse to its
lair. Such knowledge is not inconsistent with his healthy
abomination of uncontrolled enthusiasm in the critic;
though both drama and criticism of it are written by artists, the first may be hot, but the second must be coldly
calm. Nathan casts a dubious eye in the direction of the
critic whose style has too evidently preoccupied him.
" There is a type of critic who thinks primarily in terms
of literary composition. When he sits down to record his
findings he concerns himself not with recording his findings so much as with recording his own talent as a writer
of prose. What results is neither criticism nor literature."
It is not, then, that Nathan lacks emotionalism; it is
that he is on guard against it, — reins it in with so success-

ful, often too successful a control that it is self-criticized into highly intellectual merriment. He is less a creature of ambivalence than is Mencken; in the matter of the theatre, however, the truth breaks out. Ridicule it as he may, he loves it, slap-stick, bladders, footlights, tights, dilapidated scenery, tottering mummers and all. He is chained by love to the things he hates, and derives his diversion from the inevitable conflict and resolution. Uncommitted as he is to a program, cherishing no belief in purpose or certainty, an enemy to pretense in whatever guise, it cannot be said of him that any faith unfaithful keeps him falsely true.

As his mistrust of the emotions is allied to his fundamental dubiety, so to these is allied his gift for pricking the bubbles of art. There are times when his mistrust of the emotions suggests a fear of them; he has often been unjust to lyrical expansion. Yet who has better appreciated the poetry of a Rostand's *La Dernière Nuit de Don Juan?* And how many paragraphs of illuminating criticism have been packed into his bold epigram on Sir James Barrie, — "the triumph of sugar over diabetes"?

It is such frivolity as this that leads academic minds astray in their evaluation of Nathan. The falsely dignified professoriate that he so heartily abominates might more readily accept the attitude were it to appear with decency as "cosmic indifferentism." Nathan prefers not giving a damn to being cosmically indifferent. Yet this is not the whole story. Such an indifference would logically subside into sterile silence. In Nathan it expands into wordy music because, being a confessed hedonist, he finds his special pleasure in playing endless variations upon the basic theme.

As for Nathan's protestations of insincerity, his fondness for paradox misleads him into misleading his readers. When he inveighs against the quality of mere honesty in critics, he is more precisely inveighing — as Mr. Darlington has seen [1] — against the ignorance of that honesty; only that the English writer takes Mr. Nathan's topsy-turvy logic a trifle too seriously. He is right to suspect — suspect? — Mr. Nathan of a "tendency to be too clever"; in the realm of the frivolous this corresponds to ponderosity among the pedants. One who reads Nathan with half an eye, however, knows where the man's heart lies, despite the evidence of his dictionary. Even when Nathan tries to be self-revelatory, he lapses into the ever-beguiling paradox. " I am generally complimented," he once said to me, " with being truthful. What I am is merely honest. Who can truthfully say of any critic that he is truthful? " (Is it Pilate or Paradox who asks that question?) " I have capitalized honesty. It has been a profitable business. I have had little competition in the field of dramatic criticism, so the job has been an absurdly simple one. Some day, I shall write a chapter on the commercial value of mere critical honesty in America. Any one who practises it will either (1) get rich or (2) lose his job." What Darlington calls Nathan's occasional dishonesty is simply Nathan's eternal propensity for toying with logic, for teasing accepted

[1] *Literature in the Theatre,* by W. A. Darlington. London. Pp. 89–93.

opinion, for being "agin' the government." To match paradox with paradox, Nathan's "dishonesty" is one of his peculiarly personal ways of being honest. Some read critics for judgments; others read judgments for critics. Nathan is read not for judgments but for Nathan.

Where Mencken proclaims the Nietzschean "Be hard!" Nathan, between puffs at his stogie, drawls a leisurely "Be indifferent," without any exclamation point after the phrase. "Life," he has written in the Foreword to *The World in Falseface* (the very title implies a world become puppets), — "Life, as I see it, is for the fortunate few — life with all its Chinese lanterns, and sudden, lovely tunes, and gay sadness." (Mark that "gay sadness"; it is an image of the whole man, — his paradoxicality, his conciseness, his surfaces and his depths.) "In so far as I have any philosophy at all, it is founded upon that theory. For the Nietzschean 'Be hard!' I have no use, however. It savors too much of canon, thong and overly intense purpose. For myself, I substitute 'Be indifferent.' I was born indifferent and at forty I find myself unchanged in attitude. . . . Indignation does not make, and never has made, the world any better than has my own objectionable philosophy of contentful *laissez faire*. No great man from Jesus Christ to Stonewall Jackson has been fired by philosophical asperity and spleen. Rome, the greatest nation in history, was never indignant about anything. Nor has been or is the nation of tomorrow, Japan. The chronic indignation of France is rapidly driving her onto the rocks."

The man's underlying sincerity, as distinguished from

his frequently wilful toying with words and phrases, is attested by the contradictions that one may discover in his pages. Now he seems to favor the closet drama; now he ridicules the notion that plays are to be tested anywhere except on the stage. Here he proclaims a life of pleasure; there he is hard put to it to tell what pleasure is. He defines nincompoops in terms which, in the very next sentence, include him in the definition.

Such indifferentism instinctively avoids loyalties and allegiances, which are in themselves connotative of a comparative certainty. Nathan belongs neither to the " younger " nor to the " older " generation; by present years as by independent outlook he stands apart from both. He is as wary of the newest " ism " out of Greenwich Village as of the oldest " ology " out of the university corridors.

In all his criticism there is at once an impishness and a deeply underlying sobriety. He is, thus considered, not so much an imp of the perverse as an imp of the inverse. I am not toying now with words. Nathan's fondness for topsy-turvy contemplation, evident from the very structure of his favorite turns of phrase, springs from the roots of his character. His gift for elucidation by inversion is in itself a profound comment upon life and letters.

" An idea, on whatever subject " (I quote again from the Foreword to *The World in Falseface*) " seems to me to be more in key with my attitude toward life if it is predicated upon an art. I like the notion of that kind of ideational genealogy. Art is, in the view of nine tenths of the human race, bootless, ' unpractical.' Thus, whether good or bad, art provides an admirable postulate for my philosophical snobberies. Life, to me, is artificial; all my criticism of the drama is based on the theory that drama is artificial life. There isn't so very much difference, in my way of looking at things, between life as it actually is and life as it is shown in the theatre. I have often been accused of this attitude by critics of my criticism, and have often been lambasted for it; I plead guilty to the charge. The theory that drama while admittedly mimicking life yet in some esoteric way departs violently and absurdly from life is maintained chiefly by persons whose life departs violently and absurdly from the drama. ' That isn't true to life,' said the Harlem shoedealer, as he watched ' Lord and Lady Algy.' ' That isn't true to life,' echoed the flapper, as she watched ' Rosmersholm ' . . ."

Note that the emotion mistrusted by Nathan is chiefly the emotion of the mob. The aristocrat of intelligence (which is not always synonymous with the intelligentsia) views life with a higher emotional response undreamed of by cobblers and flappers, — one which renders him liable to complications hardly possible of occurrence in the routine existence of the herd. Yet, in the Nathanian conception, he must have an intellect, a sense of humor, an aesthetic of indifference, that controls, that does not surrender to, his emotional response.

All the world, then, to Nathan, is a stage, and he the critic thereof. At one and the same time it must be real and make-believe, the footlights serving as the sign of equality in the equation established between the play-house and life.

3. Drama as the World — The Critic as Showman

Consonant with his views of the world as theatre, Nathan regards himself as critic in the light of a show-man who, in addition to talking sense, must provide for his readers an interesting and attractive spectacle. Rapier thrusts alternate with the crack of the slap-stick. The title of his second book — *Bottoms Up* — symbolizes strikingly two of his salient attributes: his topsy-turviness and his unremitting indecorousness. " An application of the slap-stick to satire," runs the sub-title of what Nathan now refers to as " this low joke-book." And surely, when one read it, the first impulse was to turn the author bottom up and make more literal application of the slap-stick. Call it indecency if you will; I behold in it a wholesome, if by no means the only, attitude toward the universe. That title, by the way, reveals yet a third of Nathan's stylistic stigmata: what we may call his callipygian complex. Is there a critic alive who in his writings has employed more numerous or more humorous circumlocutions for that unspeakable portion of the human anatomy which branches outward from either side of the *os coccyx*? Unadorned indecency? Mere flippancy, perhaps, — phallic foolery? Very well. To me, however, there is welcome relief in this frank addition of the lower re-gions to the metaphors of art that have so long been re-stricted (by the psychological process of " displacement

uyward ") to the head and the heart. In criticism, meta-
phorically, theologically and anatomically, Nathan sponsors the " nether regions." A deep student of the impedimenta of learning, he has never yielded to critical
esoterism. Though he has written no fat books filled with
erudite commentary, I more than suspect that he knows,
far more than the professors of the drama, that drama
which they profess, — its dates and facts; its course in the
countries of Europe; all those externalities which mask
ignorance of the real drama beneath dates and data. He
is simply impatient of analysis; and this, in him, is neither
virtue nor defect, but a personal trait. Nathan is the synthetic critic par excellence. Where others — with perfect
right — prefer to preface their results with the details
through which these were attained, Nathan rarely goes
into extended discussion. For all his suspicion of the emotions, his own intuitional response is rapid. Here are no
beginnings; no conclusions; here is only a percipient mind
in flux.

Yet, since Nathan, too, is faithful in his fashion, we
may run up a structure of theory based upon his writings
and relate him to the dramatic criticism of our generation.

4. Drama as Aristocracy

Art, being the essence of personality, is by that very
fact in the best sense aristocratic. The drama, requiring
as it does for presentation the convocation of a large
public, collides, as theatre, with the mass. (I speak always of aristocrat as man at his best, and of mass as
undifferentiated man; never do I employ these terms in

a class sense.) Thus Nathan can write, in *The Critic and the Drama:*

Drama is, in essence, a democratic art in constant brave conflict with aristocracy of intelligence, soul and emotion. When drama triumphs, a masterpiece like ' Hamlet ' comes to life. When the conflict ends in a draw, a drama half-way between greatness and littleness is the result — a drama, say, such as ' El Gran Galeoto.' When the struggle ends in defeat, the result is a ' Way Down East ' or a ' Lightnin'.' This, obviously, is not to say that great drama may not be popular drama, nor popular drama great drama, for I speak of drama here not as this play or that, but as a specific art. And it is as a specific art that it finds its test and trial, not in its own intrinsically democratic soul, but in the extrinsic aristocratic soul that is taste and connoisseurship and final judgment. Drama that has come to be at once great and popular has ever first been given the imprimatur, not of democratic souls, but of aristocratic. Shakespeare and Molière triumphed over aristocracy of intelligence, soul and emotion before that triumph was presently carried on into the domain of inferior intelligence, soul and emotion. In our own day, the drama of Hauptmann, Shaw and the American O'Neill has come into its popular own only after it first achieved the imprimatur of what we may term the unpopular, or undemocratic theatres. Aristocracy cleared the democratic path for Ibsen, as it cleared it, in so far as possible, for Rostand and Hugo von Hoffmansthal.

I am inclined to question the intrinsic democracy of drama's soul; nor do I subscribe to the dictum that the drama is, in essence, a democratic art. Rather is it the theatre that is a democratic trade, purveying the essential aristocracy of the dramatic art. The play, read for itself alone, as between one artist and another, is drama; the play, presented for an audience, promptly engages upon that struggle of which Nathan speaks so discerningly. In the auditorium where a great play is being given, a subtle battle is going on. There is, on the one side, the finer taste of the relatively few; on the other, the coarser appreciation of the majority. As a result, to put the case in its barest terms, the few get drama, the many get theatre, with all its external appeal to emotions not aesthetically relevant. These distinctions between drama and theatre, between the few and the many, lead directly to a couple of the most mooted points in dramatic criticism: (1) Closet drama as against the acted play; (2) the psychology of the crowd. On each, Nathan has written with his peculiar blend of common sense and theoretic percipiency, not always without confessed self-contradiction.

Yet, for all Nathan's talk of inconsistency and inevitable change, if one reads his *opera* from first to latest, there is a fairly definite consistency-in-inconsistency. There have been no important changes of position. What Nathan was at the beginning he largely remains today.

5. *Print versus Production*

"Good drama," says Nathan, in one of the finest as well as shortest definitions that I know, "is anything that interests an intelligently emotional group of persons assembled together in an illuminated hall." I could spare the illuminated hall and even the persons; what attracts me is the phrase "intelligently emotional." Here, it seems to me, is the basis of all artistic appreciation. Here, too, is unintentional self-definition by Mr. Nathan, characteristically couched in a minimum of space. How vastly superior, for example, is such an attitude to that connoted by the definition given in William Archer's book on *Playmaking: A Manual of Craftsmanship:* " The only really valid definition of the dramatic is: Any representation of imaginary personages which is capable of interesting an average audience assembled in a theatre." Not only is that too cocksure; with the word " average " it sells the case to mediocrity. Nathan's " intelligently emotional " is so great an improvement over Archer's " average " that it excludes it implicitly and connotes an entire attitude toward all of life. Such connotation is in itself the finest comment upon criticism which, if it is not produced by and does not in turn react upon life, is a sterile and a pedantic occupation.

Drama in the library — in print, or, as it was once called, closet drama — or drama in the theatre? Let me confess at the outset that I prefer my drama in the theatre, provided always that it is in every way produced with intelligence. It is fairly safe to assume that even most pedants would have their plays represented in the flesh and blood for which they were written. This is hardly the place in which to embark upon a discussion of the origins of the conflict between the drama as a reading for the individual and as a spectacle for the crowd.[1] In

---

[1] That conflict may be followed, among other places, in Spingarn's *Literary Criticism in the Renaissance,* or in the same critic's *Creative Criticism.*

the United States, the chief representative of the Castelvetro doctrine has been Brander Matthews, whose attitude
toward the drama as production may be summed up in a
quotation from his *Studies on the Stage:*

A play is written not to be read, primarily, but to be acted. M.
Coquelin has recently pointed out that if Shakespeare and Molière
. . . were both as careless as to the printing of their plays, it was
because they both knew that these plays were written for the
theatre, and that only there could they be judged properly. Seen
by the light of the lamps, a play has quite another complexion
from what it bears in the library. Passages pale and dull . . .
when read coldly by the eyes, are lighted up by the inner fire of
passion when presented in the theatre; and the solid structure of
the action, without which a drama is naught, may stand forth in
bolder relief on the stage.

That, to me, is highly questionable. The right reader
lights up his play with an inner passion that is far more
genuine than the fires of the average production, which
are not so much fires of passion as palpably insincere fireworks. As to the " solid structure of the action, without
which a drama is naught," — that could have been written only by one without an artistic imagination. It is not
criticism so much as confession.

There is, in *The Critic and the Drama,* a passage that
seems to agree with this arbitrary pronouncement of Matthews. " To hold that the drama as an art may achieve
its highest end read by the individual and not acted in the
theatre, is to hold that music as an art may achieve its
highest end played by but one instrument and not by an

orchestra. The theatre is the drama's orchestra. Upon the wood of its boards and the wind of its puppets is the melody of drama in all its full richness sounded." There is here, I believe, a subtle confusion between drama as art and drama as production. Music, mutely inscribed upon paper, is surely not the voice invoked by the composer; yet that paper contains none the less the soul of the composer's work, which performance can mar as often as make. It is as mute as it was in the creator's imagination, yet symbolizes excellences and defects which the true musician can chart. The drama is in better case, since we are speaking during much of our entire waking existence, and speech, the means of all, is easily read from print, while a reading knowledge of music is rare.

However, the best answer, or rather complement, to the paragraph just quoted from Nathan, is provided by a quotation or two from one of his earlier books: *The Popular Theatre.*

To read a play, and to go then to the playhouse to see it acted, is much like marrying a woman before proposing to her. In reading a play, the imagination of the reader is limitless; in seeing the same play acted, his imagination is more often bounded in the front by a Mediterranean sky that nine times out of ten is rich in grease-spots and flyspecks; on the right by the spectacle of a Sinn-Feiner in shirt-sleeves making ready to shift a scene; on the left by a marble villa through the canvas scene of which one detects the stage-manager chewing a slice of plug cut; and in the back by a catarrhal old party who persists in sticking the toe of his shoe simultaneously through the rear aperture in the seat and into the rear person of the spectator. Glancing up in the library from the printed book of the play, the dreaming vision may dally, without hindrance or interruption, in the sweet fields of fancy, and there sniff deliciously the scene of imaginative blossoms. . . . Imagination thrives upon solitude. In a crowd, it is dismayed, lost. . . .

To go back a paragraph:

The person who reads a play and takes himself then to see it acted in the theatre goes never to observe the superiority (or even parity) of the interpreters' imagination to his own, but rather always to observe in what remote degree the interpreters themselves, and the imagination of the interpreters, are successful in approaching the results of his own imagination. . . . In a word, the theatre in such cases is a place to which one goes less in the hope of complete illusion than in the hope of being only halfway disillusioned.

To go forward a paragraph:

The library chair, however hard, has in it the illusion of a thousand Reinhardts, a thousand Bernhardts.

Though Nathan later wrote (in *The Critic and the Drama*) that " the criticism that nominates itself to hold drama and the theatre as things apart is a criticism which, for all its probable integrity and reason, suffers from an excessive aristocracy," we find him — not only in *The Popular Theatre,* but in the selfsame *Critic and the Drama* where the dictum occurs — virtually holding the drama and the theatre as things apart.

Thus, on page 58 of the latter:

There is the printed drama — criticize it.
There is the same drama acted — criticize it.

Are not these two different things? Is not criticism of the acted play largely criticism of acting, production, scenery, and other aesthetic irrelevancies? Nathan has given his answer not only theoretically; his whole corpus of criticism is a remarkable devastation of the stage as betrayer of the drama.

One half suspects that his refusal to accept this "excessive aristocracy" is rooted in his personal aversion to the sobriety it connotes. For does he not admit its "probable integrity and reason?" The real difference between Nathan and Spingarn (it is chiefly Spingarn whom Nathan here has in mind) is not so much a contradictory theory as it is — Nathan and Spingarn.

INTERMEZZO

Spingarn, Mencken and Nathan

Spingarn has been, to the theory of our contemporary dramatic criticism, what Nathan has been to its practise: a force and a value. The influence of Joel Elias Spingarn, indeed, has been a potent, if silent one, throughout the area of our critical activities during the past fifteen years. He is responsible not only for an aesthetic attitude which, though it owes much to the doctrines of Croce, is not wholly to be confused with them, but for an approach which is, as much as any man's can be, his own. In an article that appeared in *The Freeman*, May 2, 1923, the author of *Creative Criticism* sought to clarify an issue that has beclouded recent American writing upon literature and the drama alike. Effectively he disposed of the

" four-headed monster " that Mencken had spawned in the first series of his *Prejudices* and that Nathan, some years later in his *Critic and the Drama,* had but half decapitated. The ogre of Mencken's fancy was the so-called " Croce-Spingarn-Goethe-Carlyle " theory; in Nathan it had shrunk to " Goethe-Carlyle "; in a review of my *Drama of Transition,*[1] by Mr. Pierre Loving, it assumed the avatar of " Croce-Spingarn," — an embodiment nearer, at least, to historic truth. Yet the theory, as Mr. Spingarn was compelled at length to show, is almost unadulterated Spingarn.

The response of Nathan to that theory appears in the chapter on Aesthetic Jurisprudence, in *The Critic and the Drama.* It is a characteristic response, — one which neither accepts nor rejects. The " Goethe-Carlyle " theory, he tells us, " may, I believe, at times safely be chucked under the chin and offered a communication of gipsy ardour by the critic whose emotions are the residuum of trial, test, and experience." But what is that theory, and Nathan's understanding of it? It is, in effect, Spingarn's violoncello in terms of Nathan's tambourine: almost the same music on a different, and a giddier, instrument. It connotes, so far as this brief controversy is affected, a sharp distinction between the artist's intention and his actual creation. Spingarn indeed, might have made his point even clearer by a short quotation from Croce's immediate predecessor, Francesco de Sanctis.

---

[1] See Mr. Loving's review of my book in the *N. Y. Evening Post Literary Review,* February 17, 1923. I am afraid that the book itself was responsible for the " Croce-Spingarn " avatar.

L'arte, says De Sanctis in his *Storia della Letteratura Italiana, è realtà vivente, che abbia il suo valore e il suo senso in sè stessa. . . . L'uomo non fa quello che vuole, ma quello che può.* Art, in other words, contains within itself the values by which it is determined; not the volition of the creator but the actual spirit of the creation determines aesthetic worth.

Spingarn, while writing, some dozen years after his first book, the essays that make up his *Creative Criticism,*[1] came upon two passages in Goethe and Carlyle that seemed to reënforce the Crocean conception as the American was then applying it to the drama. " So I quoted them," he explains, in the article I have pointed out. " They were passages in which it is said that the critic should concern himself with the poet's own intentions and not with rules laid down by others; that the critic should ask of any creative work: ' What has the writer proposed to himself to do, and how well has he succeeded in carrying out his plan? ' It is one of Goethe's most casual utterances, let slip in one of his essays and never elaborated; it is repeated by Carlyle in his essay on Goethe; and long forgotten, it has now apparently become the rallying cry of quite a number of our younger critics. Understood rightly, it does explain exactly what I intended it should; understood literally, as it seems to have been understood by virtually the whole of that tiny minority which reads what I write, it completely distorts not only Croce's

---

[1] The essays comprising this book were written between 1910 and 1913. Despite Mencken's statement in *Prejudices I,* however, all except the first were written after Professor Spingarn had left Columbia.

meaning but any possible truth. For the 'intentions' of a writer, in the literal sense of that word, may be of no more concern to his critics than the colour of his hair."

(" Intention," I may interject, is an unfortunate word, — as unfortunate, indeed, as " wish " in the Freudian sense. For, in each case, a process that is largely unconscious has been labelled with a word denoting, in common usage, a heightened consciousness.)

" To say," continues Spingarn, " that Goethe and Carlyle are the fathers of the Crocean system because it has been possible to find in their work isolated utterances which seem to anticipate one of the minor incidents of his thought, is on a par with Professor Irving Babbitt's contention that the modern theory of the relation between ' genius ' and ' taste ' is not modern at all because two characters in one of Smollett's novels used the words ' genius ' and ' taste ' over a century ago."

It should be definitely established that the names of Goethe, Carlyle and Croce do not belong in conjunction with Spingarn's as the co-authors of a theory which Spingarn adumbrated several years before the appearance of Croce's *Estetica*. That theory, in essence, is to be found in Spingarn's *Literary Criticism in the Renaissance*, a youthful but scholarly work first published in 1899 and later translated, under the aegis of Croce, into Italian. In it, Spingarn, seeking to dispose of Castelvetro's theory of the theatre,[1] announces his answer that the artist, rather

---

[1] See *Literary Criticism in the Renaissance*, 1899, pages 60 to 106 (The Theory of the Drama), especially pages 71–72.

than the creature of the external conditions of his craft, is the creator of an inner life by the standards of which alone he is to be judged. To interpret it as secluding the drama categorically apart from the theatre is completely to misunderstand it. For, despite the overemphasis that Spingarn placed upon certain aspects, his theory is " concerned with neither drama nor theatre on an empirical plane." In Croce, later, Spingarn found much to support this view; he has himself been instrumental in renewing it in America. I say " renewing " because the idea is, in one shape or another, well established in the liberal tradition of American criticism. Poe, as has been shown, reveals in his critical theory some notable anticipations of Croce.[1]

The theory we have to deal with, then, is not the quadriga of Mencken's invention; nor does it answer to either of the bicapitate variants of the Messrs. Nathan and Loving. It is, if we must have a name, simply the Spingarn theory. It is so typical of the man himself and his outlook upon the world, that already in 1899, and in the later *Creative Criticism*, it forecasts the New Manifesto issued by Spingarn in *The Freeman* for June 7, 1922. Idealism, he there declares, " divides those who seek truth inside the spirit of man from those who seek it outside. And only on the basis of what is inside us can we build that creative energy of thought and faith which the world has lost, and with it its happiness."

[1] See my *Poe As A Literary Critic* (Little Blue Book, no. 730 of the Haldeman-Julius collection), pages 41 to 54. Arthur Ransome, in his fine book upon Poe, 1910, noticed years previously the resemblances which I have indicated at somewhat greater length.

113

There is no theory of dramatic criticism in Carlyle, as Spingarn has pointed out; there is none in Goethe that " categorically secludes drama in a place apart from the theatre "; there is no theory of the drama in Croce, and Mr. Walkley, Croce's chief champion in England, maintains that Spingarn's theory is wholly un-Crocean. In all these men is something that Spingarn has found useful for the purpose of illustrating his own marked reactions to the Castelvetro doctrine. The theory, for better or worse, is Spingarn's. With this, one feels, the matter may be closed.[1]

6. Crowd-Psychology and the Drama

Few factors associated with the theatre have been so misunderstood by general audiences as that crowd-psychology of which so often they are the exponent. The theatre, as theatre, finds it easy to exploit that peculiar psychology. What then? Is the appeal to the mob attributes of an assemblage justified as art because it is established as science? Playwrights trade upon crowd-psychology in exact proportion to their own lack of individuality. Back of every work of art, more important than the nation or the people that helped give it birth, stands the individual, the personality. Though as a human being he may form part of the crowd, as an artist he is its enemy, or at least independent of its dictates. Nat-

---

[1] The chapter, in *The Drama of Transition* that led, indirectly, to Spingarn's corrective article in *The Freeman*, is entitled Backgrounds in Contemporary Dramatic Criticism, pages 21 to 57.

urally he shares with them their human frailties; but he is an artist in so far as he triumphs over them and creates of this weakness his strength. The crowd, indeed, is the very symbol of that imperfect reality which the artist would not so much escape as make over. Art begins and ends in the individual. For it, the " crowd " simply does not exist.

Here, again, Nathan reacts to the problem in his intensely personal manner. Indeed, I know of few articles in the Nathanian canon wherein the man attacks a theory in a more illuminatively individual way. Note, in the excerpts which follow, how on the one hand he directs this scorn against the anti-crowd, so to speak, of professors; at the same time yielding not an inch to the theatrical yokelry. Note how, having brushed aside the academicians on the one hand and the sansculottes on the other, he exalts himself — the individual — through his exaltation of the aristocracy in the audience. Note how he achieves this through a characteristic feat of intellectual topsy-turvy.

Nathan attacks the theory of the crowd at its psychological source, proceeding to his academic task in most unacademic language:

The Le Bon and Tarde notion, gobbled whole by the jerkwater Solomons, to the effect that the collective psychology of the crowd is instrumental in reducing the intelligence and poise of that crowd to the lowest common denominator is more often anything but true. While it may be true of a crowd at a prizefight or dinner party or dance, it is worse than imbecile to hold it true of a crowd in the theatre or in an art gallery or at a symphony concert. Take the lowest type of crowd imaginable, the type in which there is not more than one half-civilized man to every hundred, the crowd, for example, at a professional baseball game, and bundle that crowd bag and baggage into some great Carnegie Hall where they are playing Beethoven's Fifth. What would happen? At first, undoubtedly, a great deal of loud snickering and oh sassafras and bandying of sour *mots* and let's get the hell out of this morgue, and what then? A slowly settling mass, a crowd gradually — very gradually perhaps — accommodating itself to its accursed surroundings, a crowd gradually shaming itself up to the conduct of its more genteel and more cultured and more disciplined component parts — and a crowd listening at length — if true enough, not entirely with interest and sympathy, at least with open mind and respectful silence.

Such a mob, instead of being lowered to its average indecorum and stupidity, as the professors maintain, is rather elevated in varying degree to its leaven of gentility and intelligence.

This, from *The Popular Theatre,* in 1918; four years later, in *The Critic and the Drama,* Nathan returns to the theme:

The fine drama or the fine piece of music does not make its auditor part of a crowd; it removes him, and every one else in the crowd, and makes him an individual. The crowd ceases to exist as a crowd; it becomes a crowd of units, of separate individuals. The dramas of Mr. Owen Davis make crowds; the dramas of Shakespeare make individuals.

Here, precisely, is what I meant when I spoke, a few paragraphs back, of art as a circuit of personality, beginning in the individual, ending in him, and taking no account of a " crowd," either in the Nathanian or the professorial sense.

For the rest, Nathan is not concerned with replacing the theories of the professors with a theory of his own, nor with defending his own observations against the charge of fallacy. " If fallacies perchance insinuate themselves into these opposing contentions, it is a case of fallacy versus fallacy: my intent is not so much to prove anything as to indicate the presence of holes in the proofs of the other side."

We have here an excellent example of what Walkley has called Nathan's *contra mundum* attitude. Nathan, indeed, in response to some inner need, is determined to be " agin ' the government," even when that government is himself. He seeks differences, schisms, disagreements, though they be specious or at best paradoxical, with all the fervor that philosophers exude in their quest for unity. That his paradoxicality is largely wilful there is no denying. To say that it is *only* wilful would be, however, to miss entirely its underlying character. Nathan is the scene of countless vague dissatisfactions, self-debates, oscillations. He loves the paradox and cultivates it because it incarnates his spirit of opposition, — because paradox toys at once with Truth and Doubt, without crystallizing into Certitude. As much as Nathan chose Paradox, Paradox chose him.

One more quotation from *The Popular Theatre* may well close this consideration. It condenses admirably Nathan's opinion of the crowd — psychology and all;

incidentally, it implies Nathan's contention that the psychology of assemblages changes with the character of the assemblage, and that the trend is downward only when the work in question propels it in that direction:

In a popular theatre, the best in drama and dramatic literature must inevitably fail. In a popular, or mob, theatre, there can prosper no satire, for satire presupposes a blasé mind and attitude, whereas the mob mind and attitude are ever the mind and attitude of a child looking into a shop window at Christmas time, dismayed at the wonders of paint and tinsel. Satire inverts the popular opinion and pours the sawdust out of that opinion. . . . The popular play is that play which pounds the sawdust not out, but *in;* the play that enthrones ignorance, flatters unfounded vanity; the play, in short, that stuffs the greatest amount of excelsior into the wax doll. So, too, straightforward psychology must fail, straightforward transcription of moods, feelings and reactions, for, save in the more primitive forms of melodrama and farcical comedy, the mob is stranger to the characters of authentic drama and anaesthetic to their impulses, thought and deportment. . . .

The popular theatre, the world over, is a theatre whose constituents are interested solely in such dramatic pieces as reflect their own thoughts and emotions, as repeat to their ears those things they already know and feel. To determine the quality of the popular theatre, therefore, it is but necessary to catalogue the qualities of the audience of that theatre.

The question, after all, stands on the fringe of aesthetics, — on that line where social taste begins to merge into individual appreciation. For great art, the " crowd " does not exist, except as it forms part of the individual's unconscious heritage. Paradoxically enough, even the most individual of us is chiefly " crowd," and the intellectual rebel is almost as much in rebellion against himself as against society.

7. *Criticism As Destruction*

" There are two kinds of dramatic critics ": writes Nathan in *The World in Falseface*, " destructive and constructive. I am a destructive. There are two kinds of guns: Krupp and pop." The epigram explains Nathan better than it explains dramatic criticism. Something in the very words misleads us the moment we employ the metaphor. It would be a boon to criticism if the useless antithesis constructive-destructive were once and for all abandoned. If, by virtue of the critic's personality an aesthetic attitude is endowed with vitality, it becomes an artistic truth. If, thus established, it shatters a previous conception, well enough. If, thus established, it reinforces a previous conception, also well enough. The belligerency of the attitude is referable to the temperament of the critic, and it is entirely conceivable that what a Nathan may establish through his innate combativeness a Walkley may establish with his insinuated learning, a Croce with his humorless insight, a Spingarn with his hard-won poetic serenity, or a Lewisohn with his aesthetic impersonality so deeply colored by personal and social indignations. Construction, destruction, — these represent moral concepts in an aesthetic realm. The critic is not concerned with results, and this, I take it, is largely what Nathan has in mind when he flouts constructive criticism. " Dramatic criticism," says he, in a chapter of *The Critic and the Drama,* playing a variation upon a famous definition by Anatole France, " at its best, is the adventure of an intelligence among emotions." Not, you will note, of a moral purpose among deeds. Hence, in art, the vivifying experience of uncertainty; hence, in morals, the deadening subjection to a self-deceived certitude. Unless, indeed, morals become, as with a Havelock Ellis or a Bertrand Russell, an art of living, not a pseudo-science in preparation for a dubious life-after-death. In this respect, it is interesting to observe, Nathan carries on in our dramatic criticism the same Poe tradition that Mencken has continued in the evaluation of our letters.

To Nathan destructive criticism is a wholesome stirring of the intellectual current, protecting it against stagnation; it destroys forms so that flow may continue; it prevents obstruction. In a word, it is on the side of motion. Nathan does not destroy that others may build; nor does he build that others may inhabit. He simply glories in function; to the academic Dance of Death he opposes the free lance's Dance of Life. Ah! But suppose he is wrong! La! So may the academicians be — as each will tell you of the other — without having had his fun or enjoyed his freedom. If they prefer the Thebaid, it is theirs for the asking; Nathan is a wayward grand-nephew of Rabelais and prefers the Abbey of Thelema. Translating its famous motto, he would render it, " Do as you damn please."

Nathan's " destructive " criticism is, thus, perhaps more than a coldly rational process, a matter of glandular balance. In other words, it fulfils a biological, a psychological, as well as a logical function.

There is a passage in the *Materia Critica* where Nathan, describing the first-rate playwright, describes at the same time the ideal of himself as critic:

It is the mark of the first-rate playwright that his attitude toward his dramatic themes is, for all his affection and sympathy, platonic. Unlike the second-rate playwright who is ever passionately enamored of and mentally seduced by his themes, this other remains superior to those themes that he concerns himself with and, while they move ahead in their dramatic courses, stands aside and lets them pass by him in review to the accompaniment of his sympathetic yet critical snickers. The second-rate playwright cries out in his recognizably typical enthusiasm, ' I've got a great idea for a play! ' The first-rate playwright scratches his nose and says, ' I've got a great idea for a play — if it be properly disparaged.'

This is, of course, not necessarily to say that the first-rate playwright is insincere, or a mocker, or a wearer of the cap and bells. What he is is one in whom the creative and critical impulses run as twin streams, one gifted with the sophistication to doubt the verity of the strongest of his own passions and prejudices, and with the wisdom to appreciate that this very doubt will the better persuade his auditors of the approach to verity of these same passions and prejudices. He dramatizes exactly neither his passions and prejudices nor his skepticism of these passions and prejudices but rather the strip of philosophical no man's land that lies between. He does not precisely disparage his thematic idea; he permits his idea rather to disparage him, at least to a degree. For, being a first-rate man, he has a first-rate man's distrust of himself and of even the best of his ideas and philosophies. That distrust Shakespeare had, and Molière had, and Ibsen had, and Porto-Riche and Shaw have now. The plays of these men are in considerable part full of that distrust, and it is this distrust that has given birth to a drama which is full, round and complete as opposed to the profile drama of their lesser contemporaries.

One can add nothing to the great dramatists of self-distrust, for they dramatize not only themselves and their own ideas but, ever skeptical, they dramatize simultaneously and coincidently us and our opposing ideas. These they fuse with their own, or, if they do not exactly fuse, at least permit intermittently to invade. The great drama is not a one-man drama but a two-man drama: a dramatization of me in terms of you. Or, perhaps more accurately, a dramatization by one man of another man in terms of a third man in whom are combined the skepticism of the first man and the faith of the second. This, of course, sounds like a mere tricky way of presenting the ancient platitude that a great play is simply a play that sees all around a character and a theme, that exhibits all the phases and all the sides. But there may be a trifle more to it. For if it were merely a case of presenting all the sides of a theme, Galsworthy would be a greater dramatist than — to stick to contemporary dramatists — either Porto-Riche or Shaw, which I privilege myself violently to doubt. There is something still more to the notion. Galsworthy, for all his ability to see two sides of a theme, cannot, like Porto-Riche and Shaw, see two sides of *himself*. There lies the difference. He writes plays the way a very competent lawyer might write them. Porto-Riche and Shaw, on the other hand, write plays the way each would write them were each an entirely different man somehow possessed of his own peculiar genius. These dramatists, like fine dramatists ever, are each of them Siamese twins of philosophy and philosophical doubt bound together by the tissue of sardonic humor. Great drama is the reflection of a great doubt in the heart and mind of a great, sad, gay man. The drama of such a writer as Galsworthy is only the reflection of a great faith in the heart and mind of a skeptic. The gulf is a wide one.

This passage, independently of the acute judgments which it contains, is important for its additional light upon Nathan's duality. As a critic, he sees " two sides of himself."

I am not aware that Nathan ever wrote poetry, outside of a few lines written during his college days at Cornell. But as surely as in the case of Mencken, his mistrust of the very emotions without which art cannot live early slew the poet in him. " I cool hot heads and I warm cold ones," said Napoleon. If, in both cases, the Corsican was creative, in the first he was the critic, in the second, the artist. Nathan himself has written that art is hot and criticism cold. As critic, he is artist as well. He, too, has his enthusiasm, his " hot " moments, but the critical fellow in him is quick to chasten them. When he offers a poetic notion in his writings, he advances it with an apologetic air. Let me illustrate with a few excerpts from the *Materia Critica*:

The notion, held by certain artists, that an artist can most convincingly record emotion when he himself is from one romantic cause or another afire with emotion is directly kin to the notion that a drunken man makes the best bartender.

123

Notice the implication of art as intoxication. Indeed, when Nathan comes to define poetry, he does so in terms of inebriety:

> Poetry is uncouth, unshaven, boisterous prose afflicted with a crying drunk. Through its empty prose head there suddenly course unsteady visions of its boyhood home, the little red school-house, its first sweetheart, and the first kiss in the field of daisies back of the old circus lot, and, passing its hand over its prosy, stubby face, it has a moment of alcoholic self-disesteem and of melancholy repentance for what it thinks it might have been and might have had — had things been other than they are — of an almost unreal happiness. It idiotically and boozily wants something it cannot have, something that, once gone, it can never recapture, and in this mood it sings its futile, foolish, groggy and sometimes very beautiful song.

Speaking of La Duse, he describes her as possessing " that one thing every great actress has had, has and must have — something that may idiotically be described as a sad arm; that line of the arm that, when extended from the shoulder, has about it something of melancholy.. The extended right arm of Eleonora Duse had in it all the tears of Tristan and Isolde."

Why " idiotically " ? Because, forsooth, Nathan has caught himself in a poetic moment!

" Art is hot, criticism cold. Aristotle's criticism of Euripides is as placid and reserved as Mr. William Archer's criticism of the latest drama at the St. James's Theatre. Brunetière is as calm over his likes as Mr. H. T. Parker of the Boston *Transcript*. There is no more en-

thusiasm in Lessing than there is indignation in Walkley."
Thus, Nathan, in *The Critic and the Drama*. Heat has
its proper place, of course. " The heart and soul of genius
may be mad," he writes in *Materia Critica*, " but the mind
of true genius is ever as clear as the heavens seen through
pine trees." There are second emotions, as there are
second thoughts. Criticism is such a " second emotion."

Nathan has the defect of this quality. In his alertness
against the seduction of his mind by his feelings, he is too
ready to suspect attempted deception. His instantaneous
detection of " hokum," however, is not solely a tactic of
dramatic criticism; in his eyes, life itself is full of " hokum."

In him, hot and cold are neither balanced nor recon-
ciled; the cold holds the ascendency, until, to add another
paradox, he waxes warm in contemplation of it. In the
same measure precisely, he extracts pleasure out of sadness; just as all great drama, in his opinion, and in the
experience of persons of taste, is touched with melancholy,
and with snobbishness — that snobbishness which is aristocracy transforming its impulse to pity into its will to
superiority, — so is the drama of life, even in its mete-
orological aspects, viewed paradoxically, superiorly. I
quote again from the exceedingly quotable *Materia
Critica*, which more than any other single book of Nathan's gives a rounded view of his critical personality. It
is significant to discern here Nathan's strong leaning toward burlesque, which is itself part of his commentary
upon life. He is not, incidentally, the professor who

rhapsodizes over the commedia dell' arte, only to look askance at the contemporary burlesque show.

The beautiful day, the day of blue and gold and sunshine, is God's gift to the plain people; the bad day, the day of gloom and gray and rain, He has reserved for the exclusive pleasure of the aristocracy. The artist, the connoisseur of emotions, the philosopher — these have no use for the fair day: it distracts them, summons them from their introspection and solitude, calls them into the open. On such a day, work and those pleasures dear to men with a taste for the sequestered are impossible: the outside beckons too persuasively and too disconcertingly. But when the world is full of wet and fog and the monotony of rain, then the artist, the connoisseur of quiet, the philosopher and all their brothers are happy. For it is on such days, while the yokelry is melancholy because it cannot be eating dill pickles and cheese sandwiches on the roadsides, or riding in Fords through the Jersey swamps, or chasing little white gutta-percha balls across the grass with a repertoire of clubs, that men of soul and sadness revel in the happiness that only God's elect can comprehend.

Soul and sadness reveling in happiness. A paradox? If you will. So is that intelligent emotionalism which lies at the base of Nathan's attitude. Is it any the less real for that? Exact logic may not be a contradiction in language; it is certainly a contradiction in life. Man does not live by logic alone. Nathan has achieved in his little garden the double triumph of using his reason to dethrone mere rationalism, yet keeping reason enthroned lest his emotions run the kingdom.

8. Technique And Artistry

Nathan's attitude toward craftsmanship accords with this intelligent emotionalism. The rational man in him admires fine construction. He is not, however, deceived — like so many college instructors — into evaluating expert craftsmanship in terms of artistic completeness. The well-made play is not necessarily the whole-made play. Nor does Nathan, for all the rational pull at his irrational emotions, rein them in so tight that they stifle. It is the great triumph of the intellect voluntarily to establish its secondary position in the arts. That the drama contains, *ipso facto*, few ideas or none at all, is an axiom of the Nathanian critical canon, and the man's critical faculties are never so alert as when pricking the intellectual pretensions of the drama. If, in his emotional honesty he exposes the hollowness of the later Maeterlinck, in his intellectual honesty he points out, as few critics the world over have done, the essential weakness of such an " intellectual " drama as Pirandello's. " Pirandello's dramatic themes are thus ever more interesting than his thematic dramas." There in a typical inversion, you have an admirable critique. Consider, too, also from the *Materia Critica*, this tidbit on Galsworthy:

It is the purpose and technic of Galsworthy to intellectualize the Pinero drama. The result, though not always entirely successful — since the intellectualization too often gets in the way of the drama — is at least entertaining. For even on such occasions as one does not admire a Galsworthy play and is aggrieved by the author's habit of placing his most serious personal convictions in the mouth of a comic character, thus making his audiences believe that he does not consider them to be as important and weighty as actually he does consider them, one has always a comfortable feeling of welcome relief that what one is seeing and what one is listening to is the product of culture, experience and a practiced taste. In addition, though Galsworthy sometimes makes a considerable ado over subjects that everyone else has already long before agreed upon, it is always more pleasant to listen to an intelligent man saying nothing than to an unintelligent one trying to say something. Galsworthy frequently says nothing, but he generally says it persuasively, charmingly, inoffensively, and very agreeably.

It is in dealing with Pinero that Nathan offers a pendant to these remarks on technique. Noting Pinero's dramaturgic disintegration, as evidenced by his play, *The Enchanted Cottage,* and describing it as a play which, instead of triumphing over its platitude (that love makes the parties to it oblivious to each other's faults and defects) is triumphed over by it, he contrasts " blueprint dramaturgy " with the " purpleprint of a salient imagination." What is the blueprint but our much-vaunted " technique "? The purpleprint, but real drama of pith and passion? " This disintegration," he writes, in a few sentences that should be introduced into every course on drama and rememorized once every month,

is a peculiarly interesting thing; peculiarly interesting because it betrays how little, after all, mere great technical dexterity matters where the ever-changing years and times have brought with them no bounty of matured invention and fresh inspiration and marching novelty of thought. We thus see Pinero successively serving as the most devastatingly accurate critic of Pinero who ever put pen to paper. We thus see, in each of his successive later plays, Pinero reducing himself to the bare bones of his talent, a talent that was once hailed as genius. That uncommonly fine technic is still there, a skeleton in the closet now grinning pitiably and not a little desolately at all those who once mistook it for a vital philosophical study of the anatomy of love and marriage, of divorce and romance, and of profound human reflexes and issues. It breaks through the negligible paperhoop of content, does this technical dexterity, and now at length faces the audiences for just what it is: technical dexterity in strip tights — nothing more. Behind it, there is nothing — save the ribbons of pretty pink tissue-paper, and the hole.

What else is there to say? Art begins where technique ends. Between them lies all the difference that separates artistry from artifice. Art, however, is not reached by flouting technique, or ignoring it, but by *passing through* its discipline. From a different — a purer — standpoint, art and technique are one, no less than are body and so-called soul.

9. Is Acting An Art?

In the eyes of Nathan, actors occupy upon the stage of the theatre a position analogous to that occupied by the average human being upon the stage of life. They are, essentially, echoes addressing crowds. They represent " the miscegenation of an art and a trade: of the drama and the theatre." (So, for that matter, does the play as produced rather than as written or printed.) Yet acting, as he goes on to say, " must appeal to the many — this is

129

obviously its only reason for being, for acting is primarily a filter through which drama may be lucidly distilled for heterogeneous theatre goers — it must, logically, be popular or perish. Surely no authentic art can thrive upon such a premise."

I suspect that Nathan's aversion to acting-as-art is founded upon his aversion — far better founded — to actors as people. Perhaps, to people in general. Psychologically, the actor-type (with the inevitable exceptions) must be weak enough in inner character to be able to assume the externalities of any character; it represents, then, an essentially colorless personality. It is a white screen upon which may be thrown the colors of the artist's magic lantern, all the better suited to color combinations because of its own neutrality of hue. Yet Nathan's arguments are none too convincing, even to himself. For, in the course of one of his discussions (in *The Critic and the Drama*) he remarks: " If acting is an art — and I do not say that it may not be — ." And again: " If acting is to be termed an art, it is, like the living picture, a freak art, an art with belladonna in its eyes and ever, even at its highest, a bit grotesque."

Here, I believe, Nathan all but approaches the answer to his interrogative divagations. I make bold to supply it. Acting is not the symphony, it is the instrument. Acting is not the painting; it is the pigment. Acting is not the poem; it is the word. Acting, then, fundamentally, rather than an art is a technique. Yet such an answer leaves much to be desired. Nathan, as sensitive to artistic acting as a critic well may be, is impatient with its practitioners. He is content, too often, to enjoy the best and dismiss it with a generous word. His flow of lyric response is evoked rather by mediocrity than by excellence. He cannot, or will not, regard acting with the aesthetic patience of a Walkley, a Stark Young, an H. T. Parker. It is not so much that he withholds commendation where it is due, as that in the very process of praise he seems to sense, — unreasonably to fear — the danger of emotional exuberance. Acting, he avers, must appeal to the many. True, but true only in an economic sense, which has no more relation to aesthetic principle than has the economic accident of the playhouse to the aesthetic values of the drama. Acting, likewise, may face the necessity of being popular or perishing; again, however, we have to do, not with an aesthetic truth but with a commercial requirement.

The actor is restricted by the playwright's lines as the musician is restricted by the composer's notes. By that same token he is a recreator, or, as Walkley has put it, " he is his own medium, his own paint and canvas, his own brick and marble." [1] In another of his books, Mr. Walkley, speaking of La Duse, distinguishes between the truth that is the actress and the truth that is the author's.[2] La Duse may not have been Pinero's Tanqueray, yet not on this account could it be said that her art " failed in truth, for it was the perfect expression of her imaginative self. But it often failed of coincidence with her author's truth." . . . " Her method," wrote Mr. Young of La

---

[1] *Pastiche and Prejudice*, pp. 101–103.
[2] *Still More Prejudice*, pp. 5–6.

Duse, at almost the same time, " was herself." We have an analogy in the conductor who gives an excellent performance of himself rather than of Herr Brahms. Yet conducting is an art.

10. The Style Is The Man

There are numerous times when Nathan's matter is the victim of his manner. This should not blind us to the important fact that no study of him, however cursory, may safely omit a consideration of his style, which, in essence is the verbal mirror of the man. His gusto for words is organically related to his facility and dexterity in the employment of them. His fondness for burlesque effects is a stylistic commentary upon life itself, rooted in his very attitude towards all creation. His instinct for elucidating matters by standing them on their head, turning them inside out and placing them before a distorting mirror is an active philosophy of life unconcerned with much beside the material functioning of that philosophy which is at the same time an anti-philosophy.

Upon that noble instrument which is English speech he has committed *lèse-vocabulaire*. Mencken may write with witty erudition about an American language; it is Nathan, however, who really practises it. Or, rather, his lingo is at once more and less than " American "; it is rampant Nathanese. In a few years his books will need glossaries. Consider such choice specimens as *yokelry, one-building universities, jerkwater Solons, boob-bumper,*

132

boobletariat, soup-coloraturas, yokel-yanker, jake-machine, hazlittry, Rialtors. Consider such verbs as *moronize,* and that beautiful infinitive, *to sardou.* In the infinitive from the French drama, indeed, lies packed the history of a theatrical era. If, out of the *Iliad* we may get *to hector,* why not *to sardou* from France? Consider, again, such nouns as *sardoudlesocks, marmalade explosion, commercial mismanager, joy-boys,* (denoting the eternal enthusiasts among the reviewers, as, for example, — but " the task of filling in the names I'd rather leave to you."); *mezzotints* (for the colored gentry, and recalling, to me, Thackeray's " mahogany children "); *the unspeakable drama* (correct: the movies), *abattoir* (theatre!), Jack-the-Rippers (actors!), *pfui opus, dooflickus, hickpricker.* It was more than happy accident that led this unsaintly George to prick, if not to slay the dragon of the cheap sex drama with the title, *The Adventures of Phallus in Wonderland.* Toward the theatre he has retained, for all his raillery, something of Alice's sense of wonder. At the same time, he has more than a mite of the rampageous humor that led the preacher-mathematician Carroll to write those books which some children think are fit only for children. The man who versified about the slithy toves that gyred and gumbled in the wabe would have recognized a certain, if remote, kinship to this unpreacher-like and unmathematical roisterer of the Royalton.

Mencken, in an early essay upon his associate, has commented, with his wonted gusto, upon the Nathanian vocabulary. " He has hauled and battered the English language into new and often astounding forms," he writes in *Prejudices* (*First Series*), "and when English has failed he has helped it out with French, German, Italian, American, Swedish, Russian, Turkish, Latin, Sanskrit and Old Church Slavic, and with algebraic symbols, chemical formulæ, musical notations and the signs of the Zodiac. . . ."

More even than Americanisms the "deliciously intriguing" phrases and cadences that so beguile Mr. Walkley are Nathanisms. They are the prose of criticism on a drunken spree, and "even when he becomes unintelligible," as Mr. Boyd has written, "he does it as a gentleman gets drunk, without becoming objectionable." To argue from this, as Walkley seems to do, that "his criticism is not his cardinal virtue" [1] is to state the corollary of the dubious proposition that profundity is always clothed in sober garb. Nathan, to be sure, has no talents for the deeps where criticism and mysticism effect a hazy, yet a genuine assimilation. He is too skeptical of those very emotions without which art cannot be; he can, on occasion, smother sense in wit just as surely as a pedant can smother emotion in learning. It is a mistake, however, to dissociate too decisively his language from his lore.

The admiration that Walkley and Nathan have expressed for one another, tempered as critically it should be, is rooted, one may imagine, in resemblances that balance the differences. If there is an imp in Nathan, there is an elf in Walkley; the insinuated erudition of the Eng-

[1] *Vanity Fair*, May, 1926.

lishman makes him as charming to read as the intellectual slumming of Nathan makes him pungent. The Gown and the Town. There are still, in England, mistaken souls who regret that Sir Arthur Sullivan devoted himself too consistently to the form of the light opera; such as they, in our own country, if they think of it at all, may regret that Nathan never sat him down to do something in the grand style. It is to wish that he were another; it is, subtly, to annihilate him, — and to betray oneself.

Nathan's " Americanisms " (read *Nathanisms*) are the very voice of his outlook. And so, to stretch a hand across the sea, are Walkley's paragraphs most delightfully laden, not with Anglicisms but with " Walkleyisms." Nathan without his coruscations of sallies, exaggerations, puns and paradoxes would be as disconsolate as Walkley bereft of Croce, Samuel Johnson, the French language and the Stagirite. The New Yorker has chosen to make of his criticism not grand opera, not oratorio, but burlesque and opera comique.

Take, as an example of verbal gusto, which at the same time does not cease to be valid criticism, his remarks upon Eugene O'Neill in *Materia Critica:*

Whenever, as in the case of such of his plays as ' Welded ' and ' The First Man,' Eugene O'Neill tries on the whiskers of Strindberg, the results are singularly unfortunate. Following the technic of Strindberg, O'Neill sets himself so to intensify and even hyperbolize a theme as to evoke the dramatic effect from its overtones rather than, as in the more general manner, from its undertones. His attempt, in a word, is to duplicate the technic of such a drama as ' The Father,' the power of which is derived not by suggestion and implication but from the sparks that fly upward from a prodigious and deafening pounding on the anvil. The attempt, as I have said, is a failure, for all one gets in O'Neill's case is the prodigious and deafening pounding. The sparks simply will not come out. Now and again one discerns something that looks vaguely like a spark, but on closer inspection it turns out to be only an imitation lightning-bug that has been cunningly concealed in the actors' sleeves. O'Neill, in such instances, always goes aground on the rocks of exaggeration and over-emphasis. His philosophical melodrama is so full of psychological revolver shots, jumps off the Brooklyn Bridge, incendiary Chinamen, galloping hose-carts, forest fires, wild locomotives, sawmills, dynamite kegs, time fuses, mechanical infernal machines, battles under the sea, mine explosions, Italian blackhanders, last minute pardons, sinking ocean liners and fights to the death on rafts that the effect is akin to trying to read a treatise on the theme on a bump-the-bumps. He rolls up his sleeves and piles on the agony with the assiduity of a coalheaver. He misjudges, it seems to me completely, the Strindberg method. That method is the intensification of a theme from within. O'Neill intensifies his theme from without. He piles psychological and physical situation on situation until the structure topples over with a burlesque clatter. Strindberg magnified the psyche of his characters. O'Neill magnifies their actions.

Perhaps that is not " style " as taught in the English courses at college, but it is the sort of style that is no more separable from the man who wrote it than is his voice.

It is in his inversions, I believe, that we find the central Nathan. Here his strange commingling of the burlesque

136

and the balanced, his transformation of convexities into concavities, his general playing fast and loose with the laws of intellectual gravity, reveal the essence of his critical self. Here is the hall-mark of the man complete. Here are his pitfalls and his heights. It is a familiar — and a deadly — device of Nathan's to criticize an inferior play simply by restating it in literal terms. No comment, except, of course, the overtones and undertones of his style. In much the same way, when it comes to criticizing the American *booboisie* — its beliefs, its superstitions, its entire intellectual impedimenta, — he simply catalogues the articles and lets them tell their own sad tale in *The American Credo*. The pun, epigram, the inversion, the topsy-turvy, — all the elements of the virtuosity behind these sonatas played by bladders upon buttocks, — are an organic aspect of Nathan's mentation. He thinks, if I may put it in terms of erethism, orgastically. And as he thinks, he writes. Nathan, appreciably, is one of our few genuine *décadents*. He is, to use the word coined by the American translator of Oswald Spengler, a megalopolitan. He belongs, not to the civilized, but to the hypercivilized, minority.

Coda

Nathan has wondered what could impel a man like Mencken to waste his time and substance upon such idiotic spectacles as political conventions. In the same fashion, Mencken, in the chapter in *Prejudices: First Series* devoted to his alter ego, has asked himself "What keeps such a man in the theatre, breathing bad air nightly, gap-

ing at prancing imbeciles, sitting cheek by jowl with cads."
His answer does as well for himself as for Nathan: it
is the world seen as a rollicking, ribald show. " Perhaps
there is a secret romanticism — a lingering residuum of a
boyish delight in pasteboard and spangles, gaudy colors
and soothing sounds, preposterous heroes and appetizing
wenches. But more likely " — and here I think Mencken
hits upon the crux of the explanation, for both Nathan
and himself — " it is a sense of humor — the zest
of a man to whom life is a spectacle that never grows
dull — a show infinitely amusing, buffoonish, vulgar, obscene. The theatre, when all is said and done, is
not life in miniature, but life enormously magnified, life
hideously exaggerated." A step above the sublime, said
Napoleon, is the ridiculous. A step above the sense of
sublimity, however, is the sense of humor. When God
had made the earth, on the seventh day He did not rest;
He laughed. And ever since, His elect have echoed that
laughter.

Nathan's laughter is not exclusively Homeric. Its
cruelty is as often surgical as sardonic; it is, at times, finely
malicious, but rarely cruel for its own sake. It is rather,
Mephistophelian, which is not so strange, since the Devil
is only God surveying Himself in a trick mirror. And
behind the mirror lies an indifferent void, just as, behind
Nathan's indifference, lies a sense of that void which conditions, even determines, his indifference. " Yes," says
Don Juan, in Scene IV of the First Part of Rostand's *The
Last Night of Don Juan.* " Yes, since All is Nothing "
— whereupon the Devil breaks in, " Then let us make of

a nothing an All." George " Juan " Nathan is both the Devil and Don Juan. Life and its replica, the drama, are the All that is his Nothing; they are the Nothing that he has made his All. And was it not Don Juan's punishment — the proud Don Juan's — to be transformed into a puppet? Theatrical symbol of that symbolistic theatre which is Life!

EUGENE O'NEILL
TO
GEORGE JEAN NATHAN

Selections from Correspondence

Eugene O'Neill at Bermuda, 1926

The " Chris Christophersen " of the first letter, like " The Ole Davil " of a later one, refers to the play finally christened " Anna Christie."

MY DEAR MR. NATHAN:

I am sending under separate cover, for Mr. Mencken and yourself, two volumes of my book which has just appeared. I hope you will accept them as small remembrances that I remember how much of gratitude I owe both of you for your encouragement and constructive criticism. I feel that in a great measure the book is already yours since you published three of the plays and had the very first peep at one of the others.

Your name, it appears, does not adorn the jacket in spite of the fact that, when I suggested to Boni and Liveright that they use what recognized critics had said about my work for the cover instead of any self-appointed boost, I carefully placed some words of yours regarding " The Moon Of The Caribbees " at the head of the list. All this matter is puerile, of course; but as I value your commendation more than that of all the others put together, it rather makes me peevish.

One of my two new long plays — " Chris Christophersen " is typed and now in the hands of the agent.

143

(Yes, Williams' dilatory tactics drove me to an agent — The American Play Company.) Williams probably has it by this time since my contract with him gives him first choice on future plays. I intended sending you a copy at once but I find my two carbons need doctoring and so will wait until my next trip to New York — about the middle of the month — when I shall bring it around to the office personally in the hope of finally meeting you.

With sincerest regards to Mr. Mencken and yourself,
Very sincerely yours,
EUGENE G. O'NEILL

PROVINCETOWN, MASS.
NOV. 4, 1919.

MY DEAR MR. NATHAN:

Your letter and the script arrived by the same mail. That you found genuine merit in " The Straw " is the most encouraging boost to my spirits I have received since the play was written. Your stamp of approval gives me renewed confidence in my own valuation.

The Theatre Guild have seen the play and rejected it. They said it was most excellent but not the kind of play for their public. Since " John Ferguson " inoculated them with the virus of popular success — quite contrary to their expectations — I'm afraid they've become woefully worried about the supposed tastes of " their public." I speak not only from my own experience. Before " Ferguson " set them on horseback they had decided to do Susan Glaspell's " Bernice " this season. But now they

144

have discovered " their public " would never — And the latest I hear is that James K. Hackett is to star for them in " Silas Lapham." My God! The trouble seems to be that you can't eliminate the weakness of the old Washington Square Players by merely changing the name.

No, even Al Woods is preferable to a success-ridden Guild. He, at least, has few inhibitions. And, although I know " The Straw " stands but small chance with them, I'll have to put my trust in Tyler, Hopkins and Williams. Williams has stated that he is willing to reopen negotiations for the play in case I should not sell it elsewhere. As I told you, he was much taken by it, wanted it, but was very vague as to when he could produce.

In the light of the Guild's rejection for popular reasons. I'm sure you'll be interested to know that the Selwyns almost took the play. In a moment of aberration the agent submitted a script to them and they actually hovered on the brink of acceptance for days. They were quite impressed by its possibilities, it seems. They and Williams are the only commercial managers to pass on it so far.

I'm in daily expectation of a Tyler decision. I wish Hopkins would give it a hearing but my experience with " Chris " makes me think it's next to impossible to get him to read a play. However, I'm going to have a try at him.

Boni and Liveright are to publish both " Chris " and " Beyond the Horizon " this winter. Perhaps they might do " The Straw " later.

I don't expect to be in New York before the middle of next month, but will surely drop in when I do come.

My sincerest gratitude for your words of encouragement. They certainly mean a lot to me!

Cordially,

EUGENE O'NEILL

PROVINCETOWN, MASS.
March 12, 1920.

MY DEAR MR. NATHAN:

This is a late day for me to be writing to thank you for your note of congratulation, but I really have a valid excuse. I have been up to my ears in troubles ever since the opening date of " Beyond." First my mother acquired the flu with a touch of pneumonia; then I caught it from her and was laid up in the hotel for four weeks; then my father had a stroke and has been dangerously ill ever since; then, just as I was tottering up to my first " Chris " rehearsals, I received a wire from here calling me to return to a very sick wife! Can you beat it? If this be the payment demanded of me for the big splash made by " Beyond," then I am tempted to remark with Jurgen that " it does not seem quite fair."

Thank you again for your note. I am sure glad " Beyond the Horizon " pleased its godfather.

Sincerely,

EUGENE O'NEILL

P.S.: — I want to write you much more than this but I'm still too upset mentally, so I'll postpone it.

146

The two letters that follow were written on successive days, during an important stage of O'Neill's development. As may be seen from a perusal of them, his modesty is no mere shrinking timidity. Always, beyond his most recent achievements, a new goal stirs him into renewed activity. The letter of June 20, 1920 is particularly illuminating.

PROVINCETOWN, MASS.
June 19, 1920.

DEAR MR. NATHAN:

Many thanks for your note. It is darned encouraging to learn that you think " Gold " is a progressive step beyond " Beyond." Your verdict is the more welcome because I was beginning to have doubts about it myself. I gave Williams all my scripts of the play right after finishing it, have not had a chance to look at it since, and so, lacking all proof to the contrary, was commencing to wonder what it was all about, and whether I had at all accomplished what I set out to do.

I suppose I shall be credited on all sides with having made " Where the Cross Is Made " into a long play — yet the reverse is the real truth. The idea of " Gold " was a long play one from its inception. I merely took the last act situation and jammed it into the one-act form because I wanted to be represented on the Provincetown Player opening bill two seasons ago and had nothing else in mind for them at the time. I mention this only because I know how impossible it is to expand a natural short play

147

into a long one, and would hardly make such a futile mistake. " Gold " was always full length to me.

I wrote John Williams to be properly persuasive on my behalf in urging you to join him in a visit up here. I hope he has been so, and that you will find time to come. Putting aside the very natural pleasure I shall feel in having you here, there is for me a very special inducement also. I have wanted for a long time to talk over with you something which has been growing in the back of my head for the past year. It is an idea for future work — a scheme quite on a grand scale, and as far as my knowledge goes, an original plan in play writing. I do not mean by this that there is any heavy blank verse, soggy symbolism or bizarre innovations connected with it; but it is an idea which is so large in outline that, even having the temerity to grant one's ability for it, it will take some years of intensive and difficult labor to fill in. The question in my mind still is, is this thing as big as I think; is it worth the labor involved, and from a purely practicable standpoint, can it be done? So, standing on this threshold, I would sure like to have your opinion. At least, whether you find it worth the while or not, I am sure you will be interested.

So regard this letter as an S. O. S. — and do come!

Sincerely,

Eugene O'Neill

PROVINCETOWN, MASS.
June 20, 1920.

DEAR MR. NATHAN:

I mailed a letter to you on a trip to the village yesterday — after which I bought the July *Smart Set* and read your article on American playwrights. After, s' help me! I underline that word because my letter of yesterday might well appear to you in its too-aptness to have been inspired by what you wrote; and I do not want you to suspect, even for a second, that I would mask my rebuttal that cunningly.

Your criticism of me and mine in the magazine is sure invigorating — grateful as keen salt breeze after much hot air puffing from all sides. If my sublime head were bumping the stars askew, your acid test would sure put a blister of truth on my heinie that would disturb any squatting at ease on the softest complacency. However, I honestly don't need blistering — on that account. My head retains its proper proximity to sea level, I think. But your weighing in the balance is a tremendous lift to me in other ways. For one thing, it gives me the added urge of attempting to make you out a false prophet — in ten years or so. For I refuse to accept your serious doubt, but rather snatch at your " But it may be . . . that I am wrong," and will try to prove it to you, given the time.

In this connection, I would like to make you my confession of faith where my work is concerned. Honest confession. I am familiar enough with the best modern drama of all countries to realize that, viewed from a true

149

standard, my work is as yet a mere groping. I rate myself as a beginner — with prospects. I acknowledge that when you write: " He sees life too often as drama. The great dramatist is the dramatist who sees drama as life," you are smiting the nail on the head. But I venture to promise that this will be less true with each succeeding play — that I will not " stay put " in any comfortable niche and play the leave-well-enough-alone game. God stiffen it, I am young yet and I mean to grow! And in this faith I live: That if I have the " guts " to ignore the megaphone men and what goes with them, to follow the dream and live for that alone, then my real significant bit of truth, and the ability to express it, will be conquered in time — not tomorrow nor the next day nor any near, easily-attained period, but after the struggle has been long enough and hard enough to merit victory.

" In the Zone " — your " vaudeville grand guignol-ism " is my own verdict — but I am out of that zone now, never to return. As for " The Rope," I do believe that is sound enough, although it's a year or more since I looked at it and perhaps I'd agree with you now. But where did you get the idea that I really valued " Where the Cross Is Made "? It was great fun to write, theat-rically very thrilling, an amusing experiment in treating the audience as insane — that is all it means or ever meant to me. You will see by my last letter how I came to write it, that it was a distorted version of a long play idea and never intended for a one-act play in my mind. And, by the way, it was not " Where the Cross is Made " that you advised me to tear up for reputation's sake. You must have confused it with another I submitted to you — " Honor Among the Bradleys " — a very false and feeble piece of work which you " bawled me out " for writing — now in limbo.

To make sure of my accuracy in this matter of " Where the Cross Is Made." I have been looking up your old letters and I find this in one written in October, 1918: " I have read ' Where the Cross Is Made ' and like it very much indeed. It would please me to print it in the *Smart Set*. But I fear that the performance of the play by the Provincetown Players around the first of December would interfere with such publication. It would be impossible for us to use the play before our January issue," etc. So you see you have confused " The Cross " with that other play. I am at pains to state all this merely to show you that it was not " The Cross " you advised me to destroy.

Your scheme of measurement to the contrary, I would like to stand or fall by " Bound East for Cardiff " (with due consideration that it was written in 1914); " The Long Voyage Home," " The Moon of the Caribbees," " Beyond the Horizon," " The Straw," " Gold " — because these plays are my sincerest at different stages. They were written purely for their own sakes. The others had their contributing causes. There are so many intermediate reasons that enter into the writing of a play between the two serious extremes of art and money. Such intermediate dramas are but an instructive form of recreation when one cannot remain inactive — and it takes time to get over the itch to put everything on paper, regardless.

In the light of what you say in your article that you hope I may top my writings from year to year, your later opinion that " Gold " is a better piece of work than " Beyond the Horizon," is more than ever welcome to me.

Let me again urge you to try and make the trip up here with John Williams. I'd sure love to have you.

And again let me thank you for your estimate in the *Smart Set*. Those are the things that count. A prod in the rear and a pointing to a distant goal, not without hope — that is what it means to me.

Sincerely,

EUGENE O'NEILL

PROVINCETOWN, MASS.
Dec. 11, 1920.

MY DEAR MR. NATHAN:

I am very glad to hear you liked " Diff'rent " — and especially pleased to learn that you believe I am " edging up to windward " and making progress along the right course.

The Provincetown Players have been dickering with Hopkins to take the " Emperor Jones " uptown. He was quite willing it seems, but demanded an all-O'Neill bill and insisted on " Diff'rent " being the other play — wouldn't hear of " The Moon of the Caribbees " or any of my others. This strikes me as strange because Hopkins has never even read " Diff'rent " and can know nothing of its worth. At any rate, his insistence on that play, and that play only, made his proposition impossible for us.

152

We would have to close " Jones," put on " Diff'rent " (taking the chance that Hopkins wouldn't want it after he had seen it) and postpone an uptown opening for a month and a half in order to accept his offer. Klauber, for the Selwyns, has offered us the Selwyn Theatre for " Jones " and we can move it up at once if we like. So I think " Jones " is due for the Selwyn at an early date. I would have much preferred the Hopkins association, of course, but his proposition was too uncertain and we really couldn't afford to take the chance.

I sincerely trust the neuralgia has let up on you by this.

Sincerely,

EUGENE O'NEILL

The last act of " Anna Christie " has been a bone of contention among critics since its première. It now appears that before the play saw production at last, it had yet another name. O'Neill here seems more discerning than some of his friends who, at the time, tried to deceive themselves into the belief that the so-called " happy ending " of the play was artistically congruous. From the standpoint of the playwright's intention it undoubtedly was; the play itself, at the end, left something distinctly to be desired.

PROVINCETOWN, MASS.
Feb. 1, 1921.

MY DEAR MR. NATHAN:

Your criticism certainly probes the vital spot. The devil of it is, I don't see my way out. From the middle of that third act I feel the play ought to be dominated by the woman's psychology. And I have a conviction that with dumb people of her sort, unable to voice strong, strange feelings, the emotions can find outlet only through the language and gestures of the heroics in the novels and movies they are familiar with — that is, that in moments of great stress life copies melodrama. Anna forced herself on me, middle of third act, at her most theatric. In real life I felt she would unconsciously be compelled, through sheer inarticulateness, to the usual "big scene," and wait hopefully for her happy ending. And as she is the only one of the three who knows exactly what she wants, she would get it.

And the sea outside — life — waits. The happy ending is merely the comma at the end of a gaudy introductory clause, with the body of the sentence still unwritten. (In fact, I once thought of calling the play "Comma").

Of course, this sincerity of life pent up in the trappings of theatre, is impossible to project clearly, I guess. The two things cancel and negate each other, resulting, as you have said, in a seeming H. A. Jones compromise. Yet it is queerly fascinating to me because I believe it's a new, true angle.

154

One thing that I realize, on a rereading of the last act, is that I haven't done enough to make my " comma " clear. My ending seems to have a false definiteness about it that is misleading — a happy-ever-after which I did not intend. I relied on the father's last speech of superstitious uncertainty to let my theme flow through — and on. It does not do this rightly. I now have it in my mind to have the stoker not entirely convinced by the oath of a non-Catholic although he is forced by his great want to accept her in spite of this. In short, that all of them at the end have a vague foreboding that although they have had their moment, the decision still rests with the sea which has achieved the conquest of Anna.

Do you think this would help — in the way of holding up the theme at the end? I sure pine to talk over this play with you, but just how soon I will be able to get to town again is uncertain.

My sincerest thanks for your letter!

EUGENE O'NEILL

PROVINCETOWN, MASS.
Feb. 5, 1921.

MY DEAR MR. NATHAN:
I am darn glad to know you think I may have found my way out in " The Ole Davil," and I will get to work on it at once.

The play is at present held by Tyler under the old " Chris " contract but, unless he elects to pay for a large number of performances contracted for but not given during the past year, the rights will be forfeited back to me the first week in March. I hardly think Tyler will go to this expense. He is having enough trouble trying to get on "The Straw" before he forfeits that too.

If you will mention the play to Mr. Hopkins, it will be a great favor. I would certainly like him to read it and have instructed my agent to send him the script. But I suppose he is too busy with Macbeth just at present to think of anything else. That goes on on the 17th, doesn't it? Perhaps after that he will have free time, and by then I will certainly have completed my revision of the end.

I hear the critics on the dailies have "crawled my frame" for "Diff'rent" uptown thereby fulfilling your prophecy that they would soon about face. Well, this is rather reassuring. I had begun to think I was too popular to be honest; but this sort of spanking convinces me that, right or wrong, I am right.

All best wishes,
Sincerely,
EUGENE O'NEILL

The play referred to in the next letter is " All God's Chillun Got Wings."

PEAKED HILL BAR, PROVINCETOWN, MASS.
Thursday, Dec. 1923.

DEAR NATHAN:

Well, I've got it done — long-hand first draft — and I'm immensely pleased with it, but — here's the rub: it's a good deal longer than I thought, as long as " The Hairy Ape " perhaps — no, not that long but longer than " Jones." But here's another thing — it is in " Two Parts " —— very definitely so — and might be printed that way. I couldn't keep it shorter, the idea crowded right out of a one-act form. I've had a great splurge of writing it — 8 to 10 hours a day —— and, whate'er befall, it's been great sport.

I hope Mencken and you will like it. I think I've done the right thing by an intensely moving theme and that the result has a real beauty which gives it a blessing.

All best to you both. I'll get it typed as soon as I can possibly get hold of someone to do the job — show it to you and make revisions afterwards. I hope to be down soon for " Fountain " rehearsals. No call yet. This in much haste.

EUGENE O'NEILL

We have found the early O'Neill lacking in respect for the Theatre Guild; now we are to discover him speaking a good word for David Belasco. Once again, O'Neill comes to his own assistance as a critic. And once again he is in his characteristic fine fettle, bubbling with new projects.

"Campsea"
South Shore, Paget W.,
Bermuda.
March 26, '25.

Dear Nathan:

I've been meaning to write to you ever since we arrived here in December to explain why you never got the script of " Marco Millions." At the last moment, before sending it to you, I reread and decided to rewrite and condense the two nights of play into one long night. The new scripts have been typed and I wrote Madden some time ago to send you one. I'll await your judgment with great interest. Belasco has bought the play and promises to spend the small fortune required to do it right. Give him his due, I think he is about the only one of the lot who would.

The " Desire " censorship mess has been amusing, what? It has a background of real melodramatic plot — the revenge of Banton's enraged Southern Nordic sensibilities on the author of " All God's Chillun " (which he tried so hard to stop, and couldn't " make it ").

What I think everyone missed in " Desire " is the quality in it I set most store by — the attempt to give an epic tinge to New England's inhibited life — but, to make its inexpressiveness practically expressive, to release it. It's just that — the poetical (in the broadest and deepest sense) vision illuminating even the most sordid and mean blind alleys of life — which I'm convinced is, and is to be, my concern and justification as a dramatist.

158

There's a lot of poetical beauty in "Marco's Millions," I think you'll find. But there the poetic is more or less obviously called forth by the theme and background. It's where the poetic is buried deep beneath the dull and crude that one's deep-seeing vision is tested.

However, I didn't start this letter with any view of boring you by an expounding of inner principles. It was rather to recommend Bermuda to you as a place to "Take the waters" in case you're planning a spring vacation. The climate is grand. There's absolutely nothing interesting to do, and the German bottled beer and English bottled ale are both excellent. And the swimming is wonderful, if you like such, which I do above everything. It has proved a profitable winter resort for me. I've gotten more work done than in the corresponding season up north in many years. The frost and hard cider of too many successive New England winters are slowly being rendered out of my system. I've just finished a devastating, crucifying new one called "The Great God Brown," which I think marks my "ceiling" so far, and I feel right cheerful!

All best to Mencken and yourself. Consider Bermuda.

Sincerely,

EUGENE O'NEILL

P.S.: The Fountain is again postponed, the delay in completing the new Guild theatre being the reason this time. A play with a jinx attached, I'm afraid!

" BELLEVUE "
PAGET EAST
BERMUDA
April 17, '26.

DEAR NATHAN:

I anticipated the Miller verdict — but not the rejection of Hopkins, the news of which reached me in a note from Madden by the same mail as your last. My hope was that Arthur might take it on, especially as Bobby Jones is so keen to do the sets. His reasons for a negative I haven't heard yet — he is extra uncommunicative with agents! — but Madden says he is writing me, and that he admitted ' Marco ' was fine writing. At all events, that is that. Harris, I believe, was impressed but unwilling to tackle such a new proposition on his own.

As for Selwyn, I really know so little about what he does and how he does it that my opinion is worthless. An interview he gave out in London in which he con-demningly pooh-poohed my plays and said not one of them had ever made any money — a rather startling statement in view of that fact that no less than six (" Brown " will be the seventh) have had runs in New York of over one hundred performances within six sea-sons (and comparatively few of these performances were given in the P. P., too!) — rather prejudiced me against him. Besides being what he must know was a lie, such spoofing in a foreign land by a brother playwright is not cricket. Perhaps I am unduly irritable about the " regu-lar " theatre cant on how nothing that pretends to art

160

can make a dollar. There is too much inferiority and envy peering through the busted seams of that old dogma of Managers and Lambs. One reason for my disgust is that I honestly believe the propagation of that theory has done a lot to discourage writers of real sensibility — but who must live — from ever tackling the theatre. And in my case, the notion is completely refuted. I must confess to having made a darn good thing out of my plays financially — a much better thing for the six years, I am confident, than nine out of ten of the professional crafty playwrights of gamblers' guesses at trade goods! Why, even one of my sailor one-acts (In The Zone) with a large cast, all men, no love interest, no star, ran successfully as a headliner for from 30 to 40 weeks on the Keith and Orpheum time and paid me good royalties — on which I got married! — way back in 1918! Knowing vaudeville, what greater triumph for the serious playwright can the ages offer? It is true rumors occasionally reached me at the time that the direction had my cockney stop the show at a crucial point to do a specialty hornpipe and sing "The Old Kent Road," that my Irishman had a few of Jimmy Thornton's stories arranged in his part, etc., but — well, you cannot prove it by me for I never saw it.

I seem to have gone off on a tangent. Aside from the above, Selwyn is O.K. to me but my inner hunch is he wouldn't look at it with any considering eye. How about Dillingham? Or Ames? They have the money, I know, but have they anything else? Do you know of their possibilities? I might try Gest. Or perhaps Walter Hampden — although I have him in mind to submit my Lazarus play to, when completed.

We are sorry about your not coming to Bermuda this year. Still, if your London plans are still unfixed, will keep on hoping.

Much gratitude for your efforts on behalf of " Marco " !

EUGENE O'NEILL

P.S. My felicitations to Comrade Mencken! It's a case of hands across the continent — while they are at him in Boston (where they have refused to allow " Desire " to play, by the way) they are climbing my frame in great shape out in Los Angeles — for having my Abbie appear in a flannel nightgown, no less! There ought to be a grand quote for Americana in that trial out there as reported in the L. A. papers.

The following letters refer chiefly to " Marco Millions," a high comedy as yet unproduced.

BELLEVUE
PAGET E., BERMUDA
May 28, 1926.

DEAR NATHAN:

What you can do now which would be a great favor is to persuade Ames to give it a real reading. He has had script for some time without any report, so I conclude he hasn't read it.

You haven't heard from Madden because he is waiting on something definite from Liveright who is crazy about

162

the script and is now trying to raise money to back it. This combination might have advantages. At least, any suggestions I made would carry about director, scenic artist, etc.

We sail from here the 15th. I hope you will still be in N. Y. then. Want very much to have you read "Lazarus Laughed," finished now but not typed yet, and want a talk with you.

as ever,
Eugene O'Neill

June 7, 1926.

Dear Nathan:

In regard to the Ames matter I thought it would be all right to encourage him to read the script, which he received at the same time Liveright got his but he has not sent it back to Madden or given any report on it. Also, Liveright's chances of getting the money to back it are none too good, I should say. I have been hoping to hear something definite from Liveright by each mail. I should say if Ames liked the play enough, and then should find out that Liveright had gotten in a definite acceptance before his, that he would have no one to blame but his own failure to read the script sooner. It must have been at his office now for over a month. If it were a question of sending the script to him now I think it would be a different matter. However, do what you think best. I really ought to hear from Liveright any day now.

I look forward with great pleasure to reading the article in the August *Mercury*. I am very grateful to you for writing it. If nothing has happened to Marco by then, it surely ought to stir up something.

By the way, it suddenly occurs to me — I haven't got the copy of the *Mercury* here to verify it — that you got the title of Marco wrong. It is not " *Marco's* Millions," but it is " *Marco* Millions." What I am driving at is to try and get an American equivalent for the significance of the " Il Milione " tacked on mockingly to his name by the scoffing rabble in Venice who thought his stories about the East such awful lies. " Marco's Millions " sounds too much like Clare Kummer and gives the wrong idea. Probably there was a mistake in the script you got.

Cordially,
Eugene O'Neill

P. S. I notice for first time that same mistake of " Marco's " is on script agents send me. Damn fools! — and also my fault for not looking it over.

Belgrade Lakes
Maine
Sept. 3rd 1926.

Dear Nathan:

My plan is to get back to town around October the 1st. I would make a special trip down to have a talk with Miller except that I'm going great guns on the new one now, after a month's struggle over one scene that wouldn't come right, and I want to take full advantage of the favorable spell and get as much done on it as possible before cold drives me from these lakes.

I have heard again from the Guild. Their committee has definitely decided they want the play — but they could not do it for over a year. Whether I can make them offer enough advance to make it worth my while waiting so long is a question. At any rate, I will hold them off until I have talked with Miller — and particularly with you, for I'd like your advice just as soon as I know that Miller has got an actor and is in a position to "get down to cases." The Guild sale has its advantages, one must admit, although I also know, none better, the disadvantages of tying up with them.

The Actors' Theatre crowd are still in the throes of trying to raise the money to do "Lazarus Laughed" from among the ranks of their million-talking, jitney-giving Lorenzos. It will cost around forty thousand. I am getting a bit sick of these groups that never have the dough to do right by me, and always keep me worrying. At the old P. P. naturally one expected it. Yet that group managed to be a great deal more self-sustaining than those that have followed. I am afraid I shall soon have to go on a search for an insane — therefore a truly generous — millionaire and start my own theatre.

Seriously, I honestly am getting awfully fed up with the eternal show-shop from which nothing ever seems to emerge except more show-shop. It's a most humiliating game for an artist. Novelists have all the best of it. But I'm beginning to sound like Benny Leonard "panning" prizefighting!

I suppose I'll hear indirectly from Miller what Hunter decides. Do you think he could do it? I haven't seen him since "Clarence." All best!

EUGENE O'NEILL

EDWARD GORDON CRAIG
TO
GEORGE JEAN NATHAN

Selections from Correspondence

EDWARD GORDON CRAIG FROM A PORTRAIT BY HUGH THOMAS

DEAR MR. NATHAN:

A copy of your book on the Theatre has come here —
I have read it through and enjoyed and marked much of
it. I like so much the amazing Americanisms —

I had a note on "applause" (under the name of
Adolphe Furst) in "Mask." *Volume I. Page 247.* Not
unlike yours on the same subject. After having read
your book I sent for your portrait and was surprised to
find you so young a man. I wish you the best of success.

I suppose you know "The Mask." Are there any
publications you would like me to send you from here
that you have not got. There are one or two of interest
— not periodicals but things to do with the new movement are here. That same '*new movement*' is playing
the ass. I am not disheartened by its behaviour but it
seems a little silly. The big men in it are practically all
united. I hear from most of them regularly and if we
looked at it from our own point of view we should have
no regrets. But the hundreds and even thousands of
new comers all of whom seem bent on copying some 10
year old scrap which one of us gave out at the time are
rather unsatisfactory.

Examples: — Knowing of the existence of "The
Mask" they fail to ring it up on the phone. For what
reason they fail to ring us up is hidden. They fail to
get into real touch with any of us so far as I can gather

from the others — Of the few men I know of in the States some are continually in correspondence with me — but not more than four or five at most — That is not enough I feel. Men in colleges who are keen masters and pupils alike seem not to realize that I have been at work for close on 25 years *for them,* not for myself. Had I played the game of self I'd have been a very rich and pompous person today —

And I do think they ought to be got to realize that some of us over here in Europe, having given so long a labour to the work, are beginning to wonder whether it wouldn't be twice as practical to wait no longer for the followers, but go ahead, make the millions alone and enjoy it alone.

I take it that most of these new movement fellows are hard up — I hear from MacKaye who tells me he finds it hard to make ends meet — and the look of the " Little Theatres " is a hungry look. I also take it that I personally could butter the bread of at least 500 of the members of this movement including stars — professors in colleges — students and whoever you can think of. The Drama League too. . . . What does it think it is doing — I take it it's doing without grub. The 10 or 12 colleges who make attempts to touch Drama & Theatricals — The solemn " Congresses " — " Masques " and what not. There must be at least 20,000 people at work — doing nothing. It is much the same here — everyone, after 2 hours experience of a stick of grease paint, wants to take a theatre or write an essay on the True spirit of the Drama etc. —

You could do us all a good by reminding these fellows that the practical way to set to work is to get to know each other and then to make united efforts, not little hole-in-the-corner explosions.

Example: A new magazine of The Theatre is promised or threatened from the States. A 1. BUT wouldn't it have been a sane thing for the promoters to have written over here to " The Mask " and to me and one or two others and seen whether we couldn't join forces.

I have been trying to arrange for " The Mask " to appear in an American dress and was told no such Journal could be thought of just now. After that it was that I heard of the new venture. Do you get my meaning?

" They say " I am coming over to America — how they know, *you know.* I was invited and I sent my conditions — They wanted the biggest thing ever done — that's just what I want them to want — but I have not yet heard from them — I hear that a lot of little European affairs are being exhibited just now. And a donkey wrote to me saying it had heard that SIR beerbohm tree was going to ask me to " stage " The Tempest for him in New York. I wonder what the devil use I could be to a man who can't stage the play for himself — It is all so pitifully *small* — quality the Theatres of all lands delight to develope. What? I want a manager — *an impressario!* and *one rich man* and I'll make their fortunes if they'll do as I want — that is catch my step and " fling along Sambo " — Your book has hit me and to that you must attribute this letter —

I see today that Liebler is without means. Would he

be a man for me? I haven't one idea — I have 30 ripe ones — and 60 or 70 coming on excellently, thank you. It takes 3 weeks for a letter to get over to the States — I thought I'd say, what I might have kept, straight away.

With all good wishes for another eye-opening book from you.

Yours sincerely
GORDON CRAIG

April 2, 1919.
VILLA RAGGIO,
RAPALLO, ITALY.

DEAR MR. NATHAN:
Thank you for your letter.

1st. let me say that until ' Another Book on the Theatre ' I had read nothing at all by you, and so far as I know nothing by you about me.

How strange then to read your letter saying that you have written more about me and my work than any other American.

Let me tell you — that if you *hadn't* — your few references to me in your books couldn't have touched me more than they do.

I see a friend in you — not only who rather likes my work in a way — BUT one who loves the theatre in the way I love it — and all the family have loved it since the first savage got up and did tricks.

And now of your suggestion that I come to America. After thinking it over for quite 5 or 6 days (I even

172

fear it's longer) I find I am as much in the dark as ever as to how the deuce anyone *can* arrange it.

I'll not come to help in a fiasco. I'd not again go out of my way to help people crack the tame old joke about the impossibility of the artist — to crack that joke I should want £300,000, and a percentage.

The Impossibility of the Artist has been proved — up to the hilt. Something new in that line is to be proved. Now — his practicality, and the only thing which will prove it is to give him *power*. At present they give him £10,000 as a fee — £30,000 or so to waste on supers and limes and then bid him farewell over a supper —

In London they didn't rise to so much. It began and ended in a high tea. In Paris — Moscow — policy of white-mice. You know all this really just as well as I do.

So for this reason I am pretty much intrigued by your suggestion.

Were " a sufficiently inviting proposal " made to me would I be interested.

I would be. To produce a play or two would be to lose money — it always is — I have no ambition to show what I can't do — I am quite as keen as at 25 to show what I can do —

But I can only do this if am given power.

You know that power is not anything a manager can give anyone — nor two managers — unless of course they had over their theatres and a huge capital sufficient to last as long as it's needed.

Anyhow — will you let me hear from you.

How anything can be even approached by letter I can't see: but if you can, I dare say it's all right.

As for dear Copeau and the others oh, let them go on, full-speed-ahead to them — quicker and quicker.

I know you think so too. They are l o v e l y — what? —

To gibe at them seriously in 'The Mask' is such fun now and again — to be 'aghast' at times, such a lark — but to consider them as they speed away out of sight is not possible for long in one who enjoys his dinner —

Oh by the way — now and again certain good nincompoops who consider themselves my friends sometimes take it on themselves to call on certain true men (like you, I mean) and discuss ways and means for causing me to make productions and so forth.

I mention this so as to state that in America I rather suspect one, or perhaps two, of attempting some such foolery.

If your invitation — (the suggestion) comes from *you*, then I am as charmed as I am merry about it. I like the whole idea then . . . and I'd welcome a visit from someone sent by you to explain how the thing is to be done —

I am a quite poor man, Nathan, but I have long ago made up my mind not to budge again for anything except power — and all the word represents materially. The rest I have some scraps of myself.

I'm sorry all this has to be hand written because I am not a clear writer — there is a type-writer in Florence, but I perfer not to let even my left hand cotton glove know what my right hand is doing — so it must go as it is.

Perhaps if you have a copy by you of something you've written about me you'll send it me — I can't think it could be a work of genius equal to the flash in the phrase " his master's voice " — and so I await it with some fear. You see I read your books aloud to my son and daughter who in their own sweet way are infernally sharp and they roar and shiver with pleasure.

A thrust home for father gives these children happiness of a furious kind I may tell you.

For our house is a kind of fortress and at times we parade round it posing as besieged angels with a sort of silent cry of " Sister Ann Sister Ann is no one ever coming? Throw out a banner father and cheer things up a bit."

" A banner, my boy? how many times have I told you that display in art is as vulgar as it is in Life . . . ? "

" But in Death, father . . . ? " . . . " Don't interrupt me, by son — and besides go and put on your uniform at once — the one with the pink and green lapels — and never again forget that in art, as well as in Life, Display is an essential — I have done."

Thus our life passes here — mostly in talking to fill up what begins to look suspiciously like a stage wait!

Every good wish to you from

GORDON CRAIG

and please to drop the Mr. as they say in the English.

June 16, 1919, ROMA

DEAR NATHAN:

You may be sure I'd love to come to America — and my coming to Rome is not unconnected with seeing you in New York as all Roads lead from Rome — and that needs no demonstration.

They will it seems recommence my school here — " School " means a workshop, a centre for me. You knew it meant a lot of other things but that principally.

From Rome I will send out far and wide — and occasionally go out myself and on one of these voyages I shall fly to New York.

Your letter of May 23 about Hopkins and yourself discussing it over (my visit) does me proud — because I know one of the speakers — If I could have chosen an advocate from all the Americans I know — and don't know — I'd have chosen you because of your views — your whole build — and your tremendous pluck.

Those other fellows all over the pea (as you no doubt somewhere describe this bit world) are a lot of piddling good fellows tepidly keen about art and theatre of any safe kind — provided they can find the right clichés in which to make it vague in a book. — Vague unpractical kind sort of suicides — Almost fanatics — and there is no madman so dangerous as that sane kind.

You saw one of their manifestos I suppose — John Corbin and his " mad if not medically " . . .

The Romans have enjoyed that immensely — and all the more on my explaining that it was all writ in order

176

to boom the imitation goods of my tenth-rate disciples. It's a lovely thought to think of New York preferring a forgery to a genuine work. *Asking* for fakes —

You are right Nathan — and *if* I was still *buried* in Italy it would be nonsense, but it's the third day you know and I have risen in Rome and Rome has risen to me.

Piano — piano — ! as they say here when they mean business.

I meet a number of excellent Americans here — some of the sweetest and best of princesses here are Americans — and such fine ladies too. One or two at the Embassy here are excellent men — And I am to be seeing an Irish-American impressario who is taking the Papal Choir to America — one called Slavin — and if an opportunity occurs I shall ask him to see you for me.

The Papal Choir is the second best thing to be found in Europe today if you will excuse me from mentioning the first.

Do you know about music — I don't — but like Zuleika Dobson " I know what I like " and when this choir of 50 voices (*no* instruments) starts off with a motet or a wail by Palestrina — Vittorie or Ingenire — then I become aware that I am a wonderful person — that being the first thing a great work of art says to everyone I take it.

There is a great strike on here — no writing paper to be got so excuse a leaf from my writing book.

Vance Thompson! that's the name I was trying to remember — one of the men at the Embassy — an excellent man.

I hope you will remember to send me one or two of the things you have written about my work — for I should value them. I was glad to see that Knopf reprints what I wrote of your book. — As a rule I regret whenever I say I like a thing and dislike to see it reprinted — but in your case this is not so — and I am ready to say it again.

Yours
GORDON CRAIG

October 21, 1919.
VILLA RAGGIO.

RAPALLO, ITALY

MY DEAR NATHAN:

I've just had a bout with typhoid fever — lasting 23 days — that has left me in a state of flop. . . . I can move and write a bit — but have to stay in bed — you may know all about it — if so you know —

Your letter of Oct 3 reaches me today. I wrote you no letter about the visit to the States for I saw nothing definite to answer in your last 2 good reports —

I am very unwilling to go *anywhere* — not merely because I still taste medicine but because and because and because — fill every possible reason in for me like a good man —

About the States — and my visit — Oh yes the States are the States, of that I am aware — seriously and keenly alive to all that it means — the new world — I know — ! but, Nathan — the " Theatre " therein and the " mana-

gers " — ? ? ? Really what *are* these? and what have I
in common with a single " *Theatre* " or " Manager " and
their damned inverted commas be he and it. American, English, Japanese or even Parochial — I come
to turn them OVER not to prop them up. Well
then? . . .

All along I've wondered when you were going to allow
me to make a suggestion as to what I hold to be the one
and only method for bringing me to the States.

Nathan — writing is *impossible* — If my visit is
worth a dime it's worth someone coming over to discuss
the whole matter — and it would be better that the said
ambassador (quite the theatre language, what?) should
come armed with some authority and backed by the support of people OUTSIDE the theatre and its tangle-
foot paths —

My fancy is, a visit backed by a Morgan — Rockefeller
— Wilson — Nathan — (even good souls like Otto
Kahn are a bit limited). Fancy for example my arriving
in America brought there by Clayton Hamilton — ! I
see him — button-hole — camelia — yellow gloves and
all —

No — I am coming with Nathan — the Extremist —
the man who has no time to waste on button-holes and
gloves — good — but what the deuce Hopkins, Jopkins
and those other " brothers " have in common with G. J.
Nathan is not clear to me — I see *nothing whatever in
common.*

No. I should burst their little theatres during the 1st
rehearsal — They are all too small and pompous for

179

me — I'm sure you are right in saying Hopkins is a good fellow and keen about my work and ideas — but there are 3,742 of such men keen about it too — of that — who doubts — ?

Why Reinhardt has proved the point — and Reinhardt is an excellent theatre " manager " —

No, what I need is simpler and safer 1. *the Money* 2. *the man* 3. *time:* and you shall then have the goods. By money I mean backing of responsible moneyed men: backing not for a season or two, but as an inventor of a new flying ship or a patent food gets backing — *the business put on its feet for good and all.*

The men — by this I do *not* mean a lot of dear old theatrical fossils — in fact I doubt much if a single theatre man would be amongst my workers — (pinch of salt needed here!) but by the men I mean very wide-awake fellows — and picked from strange places — The Time — As long as it takes to get ready — I make no contracts about time — when it's ready I open the doors, — not an hour earlier —

Now all this is inadequate to make clear to you what is in the back of my head — How I wish you were here — staying with me in Roma for a couple of weeks seeing the *one* city of Europe (Constantinople is in Asia) and not too hastily and not too slowly getting at what I want and what is the only thing to do.

First of all I'd get you to join me; we'd fix up a fine big contract for life — " Smart Sets " can easily do without you — You would be there to tell me what I wasn't to do — one's wiser half — that infernal nuisance —

At least so I imagine it — you'd not mind if I didn't listen to you every time you objected —

I have talked enough — Tidy my letter up for me like a good friend — give it more consideration than its emphasis would seem to deserve for it — and write to me as soon as you may.

Your friend
E. G. C.

ROME, Jan. 12th 1920.

DEAR NATHAN:

I received a letter dated February 28th 1919 prophetically foretelling my recovery from typhoid — It's marvellous — I recovered, yes, and what's more I had typhoid. — How you could see it all coming along and going as you did is only another sign that you always are a born dramatic critic and can smell a catastrophe and an anticlimax nine months away.

Getting well is good comedy, but once well all turns to a frost. It's like Peace— anyday — One expects so much and all that happens is back we go to the old state.

Don't let anything I write you about the proposed trips to the States disturb you a bit, merely take no notice of what I say — When the time comes it wont be a 4th class visit or even a second class one. It will be what we call an event — What? — Well then, that means that somebody will first of all come over here and talk it out from A to Z with us — From A to Y with those here who know how to talk business better than I, and then, after all that's over and agreed about, *I'll talk Z.*

If you came over, that would *not* have to be for a few days. I'd run you round Italy and show you some actors you would say are the best in Europe. — Then you'd have to come and see some theatres — there are about 6 to 8 which are worth seeing considering; they are unique and none but myself is such a Jackass as to have looked at them. — Then, during those lunches which we could also have on our trip we could talk over the idea of my being in America. I say *being* in because I loathe the idea of a visit — and off again — I'm good for longer than that or nothing. I like the idea of a yearly, visit and a theatre over there of my own.

How such a thing could be, I believe lunch will reveal to us. If it doesn't a Toscano (do you smoke them?) *must.* —

Lunch — vino rosso — Toscano — That must reveal all.

As for letters which try to explain something. . . .

Yours as ever

E. G. C.

Paris. (But write me always to Rapallo)

My Dear Nathan:

It may seem to you that I have forgotten you — not at all — although I forgot to thank you for your sending me your play about the Roman concubines — for which I thank you now and here.

But s⌐ far from forgetting you I remember you immediately I see anyone intelligent — and if he's an American out comes the trumpet and the drum for Nathan! —

I have your book (Pop. Thea.) with me and have lent it to one or two — Many Americans in Paris just now — My old friend Steichen who beats everyone hollow in taking a photogragh — beats even old Stieglitz — Craig Annan and the rest of the gang — gang's the word I think —

Anyhow was speaking of you with Steichen and he is looking you up next time he arrives in New York — so now you know each other. We dine together twice a day anyhow and I regret you are not here.

Theatricals here comic as usual, Gaietie Montparnasse real as ever — Copeau Copeau as never before. Opera snobbish forever.

I was given a ticket by its Director Rouché, a pleasant man who agrees never to direct. I had regretted I never wore evening dress (I do you know, but . . . however . . .) "Tut Tut" says Rouché "Cher maître come as you will — a great artist is always free to pass how and when he will." Saying which the good soul gave to me 2 seats in Row 5 of stalls — one for me, one for Steichen.

But on arrival at night the seat-shower and the comptrolleur refused to allow me to pass. "You wear no tie" they screamed "He wears no tie" — and it's true I never wear any tie; it being so fatuous a bit — "Anyhow if you like to hide upstairs we will give you 2 upper circle seats." You may guess I wasn't hiding in the circle however upper it was — I prefer to have a story to tell *everyone possible,* proving the snobbery of the great Paris opera 1920 and the power of its excellent if slightly tired director.

The Shah of Persia was at the Opera that evening — tie-less — add to this that the Comptrolleur was dressed exactly like a monkey imitating Offenbach and you have it — .

My books all appear in Paris soon — in French. Rouché happens to have written a preface to the first one.

How funny this foolish place is — with its courtesans and its comptrolleurs. Let me hear from you — never mind whether you've some or no news from A. Hopkins or the Selwyn Bros: just write ahead now and again for I value your letters more when Hopkinsless —

Yours

5 May 1920. GORDON CRAIG

LONDON, 13 June 1920.

So glad to hear from you here.

Your letter about your *not* being able to come over to Italy was sent on to me.

Have been here for a month — after 2 months in Paris. I quoted your masterly summing up of the Cinema as Art to the Weekly Dispatch blokes — Even spelt out each word to them on the phone to assure no errors — and the donkeys failed to quote it — Didn't *SEE* where it was masterly — or perhaps saw too well

184

and funked it. I wish I had two or three thousand pounds that I could invite you here for a while to tackle the question of the London Press and its attitude to the life of the theatre.

It's a decent press — very decent fellows on it — and considering that I can't and don't tip the Editors and proprietors they treat me very liberally.

But they are helping to kill the nation, by spreading tosh and suppressing art. What an awful word, but you know what I mean. '

Your books are better known here since I came —

They have not offered me a theatre yet. I seem to have annoyed some actors once more — had a little informal gathering of Journalists — about 20 last week to ask them if they intended to finally place the artist in power or not? So far no reply but same old clichés appear regularly in Daily Press —

Some new books of mine arranged for here — which I hope you will see —

Write whenever you can.

E. G. C.

Off to Rapallo in 5 days.

July 17, 1920.

RAPALLO. Ligure. Italy.

DEAR NATHAN:

Your letter of June 30 arrives here July 16th — so great an improvement on past correspondence that things seem really too good —

185

You ask if I accomplished anything in Paris and London. I did — I managed to parry three, nay four, attempted attacks — and without wounding the friends who were the foes. *Rouché* of the opera — now the director — *A charming lady* — associate of the Comédie Français, *Viola Tree* — now manageress of London Theatre *A more charming lady* — a very old friend.

One and all pounced — swords glittering — banners flying — biblical. I dodged one — I smiled at the second — I looked at the third — at the fourth I made sundry passes — and I am alive. It is much to say.

Their combined idea is this. That I shall go like a sheep to the shambles — without one bleat — that I shall select his or her shamble as for the fittest fitter(?)dead — that once there I shall myself — seize knife and with my own hand — take my life.

Said Rouché — " Cher maître — come to the opera just as you are — weaponless — without a buckler — without Nathan — Northcliffe or Nevermind who — come without bodyguard — without tanks — without a staff — (above *all* without a staff) come without prejudice or premeditation — and I will put the entire Opera House at your service. In short, cher maître, dilly dilly dilly dilly, come and be killed.

I dodged — " some day (or some other evening and put a phrase at your service) I may " — says I.

Next. The charming lady. " Art — cher maître — Art — oh art — " I forget what more was really said but in 6 months from then Claudel's play the " Tête d'Or " was to be put on at the Comédie for one performance only. Would I, would I, lie down and — and cuddle the Lion of the Rue Richelieu like the Lamb that I looked.

I smiled. Art — . . .

Next. Viola Tree — really I forget what all this was about — She is so dear to many of us and we are a little sorry to see her struggling with the same problems which made a nice old donkey of even the cleverest of old actor-managers that have passed — Yes. would I produce the ' Tempest ' for her: when — ? immediately — " *Good. I will.*" I said and added " All you have to do is to bring the 8 to 10 most promising of the London young artists — and write these and all is as easy as to say Ha! " — So far I have done some writing — but have an idea that our dear friend Viola Tree does not even now know what the deuce is gained by writing — or how to set about such a job — as her part of the contract.

Last. " Will you produce the " *Bacchae* " — and " Parsival " — and I will perform in it and Duse will perform in it — and — and — I will take the Theatre Champs Elysée for a week — nay 14 days. . . . "

This from an old and a dear friend seemed to me just a little cruel. I made one pass —

Nathan — Is it clear? To you anyhow. I will do nothing until I have a theatre of *my own*. Sure if only a huge barn — my staff selected by me. Paid by me . . . their men selected by them — paid by me. My theatre — mine as long as *I wish*. Even if only 2 planks and a 2 trestles — standing firm on ground which I am free to spread on — as Irish.

1. (The wrecks of Theatre plans when the director is not able to spread are many — enough to teach the biggest fool — what I've learnt. There plunged little Barker — into the Court Theatre Sloane Street — eg:—: His notions modest. In 3 years his notions wished to spread — Couldn't — had to *leave* little theatre — went elsewhere and has failed ever since.

Law of game. Once begun never leave the spot. Isn't it?)

2. (Jacques Copeau — Theatre de Vieux Colombier. Entered so lamblike . . . with Barkerish notions modest. Anon the notions begin to stir — to swell — yes even good Copeau's Barkerish notions — theatre closed in all round — no more space — for new stage — for 800 new seats — no escape — " no tarrying there " — fiasco.)

He confessed to me — it's very hard on him — but he had not call to do it — And there are numberless instances of this modesty which begins and which comes out immodest. — My idea is to start immodest. I expect I too am in error —

News from Russia. The Moscow Art Theatre is in some trouble. The three directors 3 no more. $\frac{1}{4}$ only. Stanislawsky? Stackowitch hanged himself. Dantchenko robbed of those two is but $\frac{1}{8}$th himself.

News from Rapallo. E. G. C. — not so insane as he looks, and refreshed after late encounter with the mugs of Paris and London. Pretty mugs, dear people — only fatal to one *should one be vain.*

I *Am* vain — about my business capacity — but as a

188

member of the Theatrical asylum I am not vain — not unhappy — not happy — just the warder you know.

And I may finally say that once one learns to know the inmates of that asylum it is interesting work letting them think that the warder is the one sole lunatic therein.

Write to me and amuse me a little — I look forward to your new book. I took the " Popular Theatre " with me to Paris and London — and delighted everyone by reading them the passages I like best — the deadliest —

Tell me — who is there in London who you know of as critic who could in some way learn from you — we need a whole school of new critics and I hope you know of some men — for I'd soon see to it that your book inspired them. — They lack pluck, that's the worst that can be said — isn't it?

Yours

E. G. C.

DEAR NATHAN:

I sent you off, a day or so ago, a copy of the Foreword to my new book London Edition — As it has not yet been published in America, it is still available — or isn't it apt? — If it is apt — what is it worth to a publisher?

It should be clearly stated to be " The Preface to the London Edition of The Theatre Advancing." For I only feel like this towards my own city, which is a damn fool not to make use of all of its talent great or small.

I send you also a thing on " Poets and Puppets "

Your letter enclosing letter from Hopkins has just come. It sounds as though I might have the pleasure of going with you one evening to some real theatre — there must be one in America — some place one stumbles on — sits in — leaves — and remembers forever — saying not a word about it to anyone. That's the real theatre. I have found these mostly to be marionette theatres — all so ordinary — and beautiful — No? As though I was a fanatic . . . *Sworn* to this or that theory. What duffers our contemporaries are! — Still they do notice what I meant and what I didn't state in so many rude words is — that *Any* theatre in which I find *them* is detestable to me anyhow — any art *they* approve of insipid and false — and any thing to do with them — in any way at all to do with them — is bosh and I'm off to the side of a stream or to see a friend —

There's my whole theory of the art of Theatre on a half sheet of paper.

GORDON CRAIG

Thank you for all you say — we shall see.
I will write you after Mr. Hopkins comes.

March 8, 1921.
RAPALLO.

June 16, 1921.
RAPALLO.

MY DEAR NATHAN:
Your letter of May 31st saying that your plans prevent you coming over is to me no surprise, but an immense disappointment. I cannot remember experiencing just such a loss since I began working quite a few years ago.

You are one of the few events in the modern Theatre —
and I was beginning to believe that important things
would be happening all round from your coming here and
our meeting. I don't often care to take myself as seriously as all that — but in your case I do . . . for you are
one of the very few whom I think I could not come to
laugh at and I hope it's the same with you in regard to
me.

Too many people are interested in preventing us meeting for that to be so easily brought off.

(By the way the article on you in the *Times* was quite
good and nothing at all . . . I suppose people *dare* not
. . . you being what they miscall a *destructive* critic. I
enclose it in case you didn't see it.)

When you get back from South America why not come
over — and that without talking to Mr. Hopkins or Mr.
Selwyn or even to Mencken, although if you told him to
be absolutely dumb he would be, I'm sure. For there
are hundreds of people who are aghast at the idea of me
coming to America or you visiting England, if either visit
is to raise the dust and lead to reconstruction — as each
would.

As to your visit to England it ought to be arranged —
but properly.

You say that Mr. Hopkins still " plans to sail " and
" to get into touch " with me — I must put the idea before Max Beerbohm.

" Mr. Arthur Hopkins planning to sail so as to get
into touch with Gordon Craig."

It would make an amusing design. No — no — that

191

dear Mr. Hopkins will possibly get to Europe — may put-
ter around Paris, London and Vienna, may secure some
slices of cake to take back to America for his New Yorkers,
but that he will ever reach Rapallo or ever know how to
get into touch with me is doubtful — very. (Or am I
right out of my reckoning?)

Had you come all would have been as easy as eating
bread and butter — as it is, if he comes alone how can he
find me anything but 'incompresensible,' 'impractical'
. . . and so forth.

Well, mind you, come on before I die . . . because
anything else would be what the English call ' highly rep-
rehensible ' —

I have quite a few rare prints and manuscripts (Italian)
and books and drawings to show you — *all* theatre naturally, all Theatre. You are not interested in such things?
what? — to me they seem so packed with suggestion that
they enchant me. There are wines and things here too,
and though I am not huge at these — I am a huge smoker
— and the cigars here demand that one be able to smoke.
God seldom moved in so mysterious a way as when he performed the wonder known as a T o s c a n a — and when
you smoke one it is you and not God who does the storm
riding.

I am really very sorry that you have to read my hand-
written letters — for I do not write very clearly . . .
still I have no machine in Rapallo and no one to dictate
to —

By the way — a book for you to read: Strachey's
" Queen Victoria " — an amazingly fine piece of work —

and then to take away the taste a couple of pages (any couple will do) of Byron's " Life & Letters."

Always quite faithfully,

Yours,

GORDON CRAIG

February 5, 1922.
AMSTERDAM.
but write to Rapallo.

I go to give 5 lectures in England in 10 days — not prepared stuff but the old and genuine article.

DEAR NATHAN:

Thank you ever so much for book, dedication and all — I am in Amsterdam — exhibit awfully good and much of it. Damn *pretentious,* the collection of books interests me greatly; Solid work *there:*

Most of the *sceneries* all my eye and Betty Martin, 100 times too over-important — Pouff. Theatre projects good, only that which is to go into the said theatres not taken into consideration.

My influence does not seem to have been fatal but the theatrical artist might show a stronger physique. Bakst seems to be easily caught and causes delirium in the patient —

I spoke one evening (spoke of you by the way). M. Copeau came over to Paris and spoke three days after — two or three others about to speak.

193

Nathan — I have spoken to many men here of you — and I stand by you as the *one* man in America on whom I count, and I think we are all proud of you. There must be no two or three for us.

Yours
E. G. C.

AMSTERDAM, 17th February, 1922.

DEAR NATHAN:

I am still here wasting my time and spare cash in trying to hold this International Exhibition for England . . . as one who should tie up an Atlantic liner to a port with a bit of string.

The amusing thing is I may succeed.

Your letter has come on to me here. Of course I shall always want and expect any book in which you write about the Theatre. I am much obliged to you for the book by Mr. Mencken which I shall find on my return to Italy.

I have not yet heard from Mr. Huebsch —

I was speaking last night publicly at the Hague on Theatres of course — spoke of *you* — as I did 3 weeks ago in Amsterdam — I told them to read your books — one man may — What a victory!!

All good be with you. Don't be in low spirits — I marvel at your high spirits amidst *that* sort of thing and just those sort of prigs — Anyhow you have enough enemies to keep your fine spirits high and ever higher.

Ever your friend
GORDON CRAIG

194

VILLA RAGGIO, RAPALLO, LIGURE, ITALY.
March 23, 1922.

DEAR NATHAN:

I am so poor that I can't afford a typist or stenographer. & so I can't get the assistance I once had and need more than I ever did. Hence it is that letters do not get run off to you full of the information you ought to have — & I find it impossible to write more than 30 to 40 letters a week by hand.

I am sorry to hear so lame an excuse from you for whiskey drinking — but I suppose the influenza is dragging and so on. Now about Amsterdam. But staying on the spot — talking as little as possible — & suffering a good deal (simply because of the stage wait) I did secure for London the International Exhibition — France swore it would be hers. . . . America was certain of it and G C was to open it — (bunkum is, I believe, what they call that) and in London 3 different " Leagues " and " societies " with suave confidence crept slowly toward uninfluential " presidents " and other officials with promises of some thin air (very well worded) & might *they* have the taking of it over — the " entire control " & the rest. They were delighted finally to accept the rest. Meantime I thought that if a first class thing could be done at a first class place in London under some real sort of directors, the thing was worth doing.

I got it finally — for the Victoria and Albert Museum — known to all the faithful (i.e., the common people) as the South Kensington Museum. So it is under a fine roof

— the finest we have in England anyhow — and looked after by the State and its representatives. Hoch der Kaiser is — I believe, the appropriate toast — look in towards a kind of Ewigkeit. While doing this, Nathan, what suppose you I insisted on & in doing so naturally kept all eyes *off* S. K? I insisted that none but the actors should do this thing, and I maneuvered privately to bring the actors association and an amateur Drama League together — a certain Lord H. de Walden being president of the Drama League and having money advanced some — It was he who supported my school for 1 year 7 months and then bolted — I have not yet noticed his connection with this new little affair — because & because — go on please.

When I had fixed this up & all was agreed to by both Holland and London I retired gracefully to Italy. Not before I had withdrawn *all* my designs and models. Which sounds rude and isn't. I had heard enough chatter of machines and films fluttering for 6 weeks in the wings and I determined to pinch the budding hopes of the Cinematograph in time — Everyone laughed at me — including honest Granville Barker — " Why," they queried in voices made to grow up walls and cling there — I hardly knew why, sort of instinct, and questions always floor me. But now after a month has gone by I have received a guarantee that everything connected with cinema shall be excluded. I return my exhibits at once.

But the good and great Appia says he won't play. And spite of 2 letters I have written him pointing out that since

I, Englander, accepted the invitation of Zurich to show side by side with him — he, Schweitzer, should return the compliment when invited by London. He remains coy and probably knows what he is doing. Seems to me a pity. South K. is in despair. Well, South K should (who knows) have invited me to take the reins and the cart after I had secured such a pumpkin for them. What do you think — I prefer to be quiet here — but with *absolute* freedom I'd refuse no sound and valuable piece of work. I should have done things rather prettily. I should have asked you over to begin with — I should have conjured 5 of the greatest artists living, the ONLY 5 for me, out of a hat, & " no deception ladies and gentlemen " & it would have been worthy of South K — as it is, South K. will be worthy and the Press will not discern — *meno male.*

I should have made it Scenic. Voice. Dance. Song in Recitative!!!!! Acting from 3 places not yet seen or heard — marionettes & burratini undreamed of — masks and dancers so solemn and noble that —— but why send you to the bottle again. And I should have tried to bring the best dramatists to the fore. Shaw? Maeterlinck? And a man from Rome and one from India. It would have opened in October or later — & there would have been time for all.

As it is it will be a very good show indeed — only different. As I think they only have raised £2000 to run the show with it's a good thing that I don't have the reins. But I have the whip hand anyhow and some special sounds I make with my mouth known to the 'osses and not known by the cackling coves. You will see them suddenly gallop when I make that noise — so keep an eye open. I shall be somewhere in Venice, or Venus as the Londoner calls the place, when the show opens. They have invited me over to come and touch up at the last moments — but I did *that* at Amsterdam and to repeat a little trick looks so silly — what?

Still I may go — depends if they show me they want me to run and keep Drury Lane or Covent Garden for 10 years — Something REAL and not asinine.

So here you have my news. If you want to make use of some of it do so, but don't quote me about South Kensington — best not to even write anything — Why? What use, Nathan? You know quite well that no amount of pushing will launch *my* boat: when it's time it gets up and walks into the water. But do as you like, only don't quote me *re* S. K.[1]

. . . . . .

If you are thinking of coming over to Europe this year keep me informed by wire when you leave and your sure headquarters because I'd not miss you for anything — and I'd sooner not see you in London lest you inspire me to some revolutionary deed — Here in Italy with big things as a scene it would be a *real pleasure* for me, and I have few real pleasures.

As for my visiting the great land . . . let's put it right away and let us visit the greater land — any old theatre in Geneva or Madrid.

E. G. C.

[1] *The allusions to South Kensington here referred to have been duly deleted: Ed.*

30th March, 1922.

Was re-reading your " Popular Theatre " today as a pickmeup after reading the Englishmen on the coming Exhibition of Theatrical work at the South Kensington Museum, Londinium. You are a very great fellow Nathan and I have never known another like you for pluck and perfect TOUCH with the theatre. It's touch they have not, and pluck neither.

I intend to send you some things they write of me here (London) chiefly for my own peace of mind — it will bore you, most of it — but maybe the sheer dulness of 'em, their absolute uninformed state of mind will have a certain charm for you.

And Mister Barker's new book — what is it? I have only opened it here and there and read a page or two but I found so many of my own stupid notions there . . . notions I had some years ago — and all with their whiskers curled and nice and new — and one of two old favorites too — my school (call it a place for working in), this Barker suddenly lights on, takes a fancy to. This may, *does* offend me — for to me it was (and is) — was in 1911 and is in 1922 — particularly my need — my own particular darling.

In 1911 up to 1913 I refused plenty of ' productions ' and the other temptations (some in Paris, Rouché — *linger* with an offer to do some sillyness — Comédie F:) I refused — (quite impractically maybe . . .) because I wanted to CONVINCE all those people of my quite ordinary belief in *one* not in two. Capito. One idea not 2.

199

School as *first* step
Not a step or two skipped
& their coming to sit on the first step
as the outcast in Act I, snow falling. . . .

To this I remained very easily — and excitedly — steadfast. Easy and again not easy, for I always have unutterable physical longings for good cash! And my family makes me shiver with their devilish capacity to do without coin more than I do. My wife, my boy, my girl, I mean — Hamilton would raise his hat. I will raise a laugh.

And after all this delight for this Barker to come along parodying what I took to be serious business. — Brrrrrrrr.

In fact I think you'll find not only *his master's voice* in this new Barker tone but some notes of his own — that's the impertinence!

Some student of yours should make a little volume of comparisons, cribs, and start by cribbing that phrase for his title. His Master's Voice. But no student of yours could do it. You'd have to do it yourself.

I shall wake up *some one* in London soon — for I intend to insult them some more.

The young men there are timid as hares — incredible. Fancy harnessing hares which sit, ears back, when you crack the whip.

The collection of BOOKS at Amsterdam was good — was not bad — about 300 — mostly since 1900 — yet I hear by the London papers that it is not to be included in the exhibits in London and, add the papers, " *it is of minor importance.*"

MAJOR the fools meant — and so it is. I am trying to stir them up in the " Times " and " Post " to form a collection of their own, showing them that *without* these 300 books no one, not even the critics, will know what the whole exhibition is about. Already they take it to be pictorial stuff for sceneries whereas it's just a collection of strong Dramatic ideas — all the acting implied unmistakably. I perceive that London actors are going to be cross in a paltry kind of way.

Too tired to talk more — but glad to have had a chat.

E. G. C.

RAPALLO.
February 7, 1923.

DEAR NATHAN:

I seem to hear from you once every 6 months — Is there no news. I read that Otto Kahn has been making a speech about building a new theatre which simply clangs with the sound of his money.

I read also that the Russians really have the art of being natural.

These reports and speeches draw a picture to me far away in St. Ambrogio of a life too rapid and dazzling almost to be bearable.

I feel that to be 25 years behind the times is safer for me than to be rashly 24 years late as these sensible bodies are.   Sincerely yours,

E. G. C.

Dec. 20 — '23.
RAPALLO.

MY DEAR NATHAN:

Thank you for the new book, which I am now reading with enjoyment —

I sent you a week ago the scraps of my work — little essay on candle light — and a review — or rather trumpet blast — on my wood engravings. The pleasure of having cut a block and written an essay — how immense it is: — the pain of not being allowed to have a theatre to do my best in, how queer it is.

Stanislawsky with his *" above all not a sign of the the-atrical "* is with you now. In an essay one certainly need not be theatrical — in a woodcut or an etching one need not be at all stagey — but on the stage of a theatre I can't help feeling that it's perhaps safest and seemly to be as theatrical as possible. Anyhow the thing calling itself realism born of revolutions and breeding revolutions is a trivial thing —

It is arrived at by 36 hours worth of *discussion* and good feeling around a middle class tea table — soon it becomes ecstatic and after the 5th cup it starts scratching its head — then it purses up its lips which are still wet with its tea and says " well? " — after this a pause or two — 2 more cups of tea — if all goes well another word " perhaps. . . ." then as things are going ill a little hymn — " no. 327 ":

202

Thus Realism comes and behaves. Personally, I don't like it — I suppose New York will.

Yours
E. G. C.

In Drama as I see it — scratching — kissing — spitting — eating and the like, camel-hair brush touches are forbidden.

Feb. 22, 1924.
GENOVA, LIGURE.

MY DEAR NATHAN:

Away from my home and without writing paper — you must please to excuse this scrap of good, but manuscriptish, stuff. Yes, I thank you very much, the very handsome *Mercury* from America does reach me. The last number I see contains a play by E. O'Neill and, glancing at it, I see that like almost all plays if it is to be read at all it must be read in a certain season, when the mood is three-quarters if not full; and so I am putting off reading it till then — but *The Theatre* pages 241 to 247 go with all seasons and of course are as enjoyable as ever. I am going to enjoy (for certain) the Whitman things — but just now reading is put off for a while. I have much to do if only things like letters to people in England explaining that a year's run in a theatre of my own with capital galore has no charms for me. Such explanations take so much time if one is trying not to offend all the time, as indeed I do. They write me . . . theatre . . . money a year. . . . As well write come to dine in 3 courses, cigars 1½ hours.

And cautiously they hope this may lead to success. The more I think of it the more I begin to believe that I am possibly the best business man in the modern Theatre — there are 100 better artists — but for an ordinary practical sense of how not to play the fool in this theatre game I believe I lead by 100 miles. In London, as you've heard by now, we are making a great advance in theatrical arrangements. Mr. Arthur Collins (celebrated *to me* for having come to my exhibition of drawings in 1912 and in a loud voice starting off with " Well of all damn silly rot this is the silliest . . ." after which he was removed) — Mr. A. C. has given place at Drury Lane to someone called Mr. Reandean — a sky-sign presumably — and it's signs of the sky that are needed in London. This one has already the control of three other theatres, so it was only fair to make it a square number with the Drury Lane deal. For this 4th labour he gets the ridiculously low sum of £4000 a year — But how it was arranged at all that a progressive man should come into Drury Lane is to me a mystery. Mr. Agate each week goes on and is, people write me, now held to be the foremost and best Dramatic Critic of my land. Max Beerbohm is reprinting his own Dramatic Criticism; he tells me he is dedicating the book to me, and this is not quite fair on Agate, who will be naturally immensely cross.

I was watching a great actor last night and tonight shall go again. (A small actor of small ways but a great stylist). I have not yet bought the tickets and it is 7.30. The play — a new one — begins at 9. The theatre will of course be half empty. That's how I enjoy taking my theatre —

and it is only here where that is possible at anytime —
especially in Ligure. Nice kindly people — the Genovese
— but slow at theatres — for which I am grateful. In
Milano there are more sprightly folk. They were so
sprightly last December they invited Appia into the trap
called La Scala — He walked in without a blink. It
closed on him — ruined his projects — the projects for
Tristan & Isolde the work of 20 years — and proved
that it is best to make your own trap if you must enjoy
the delights of the mouse.

Poor Appia — it is very hard on him — and he was so
excited at the thought of the Scala!! La Scala! does one
say *die treppe* — The best of the theatre is, of course,
that it can't wait 20 years for one to frame a sentence: and
so all one's early work is but useful as a spring-board from
which to leap afresh on the night — through the hoop.
It amazes me to see Reinhardt taking his " Miracle " so
seriously — why it might be a work like " Zuleika Dobson," a thing perfect and unchangeable for the way he
seems to bring out edition upon edition of it.

What Fiorilli and Martinelli of the 16th and 17th Cen-
turies would think of this solemn way of repeating and
repeating old work of lathe, plaster and grimace, God
certainly knows at this moment.

Let me hear some *news* from the States some day.

Yours ever,

E. G. C.

Kindest regards to Mr. Mencken and congratulations.

July 18, 1924.

My Dear Nathan:

You must be kept very busy with your " Mercury "; I hope not *too* busy to remember some day to tell your readers that *The Mask* is alive again *and kicking*.

Yes, I saw Walkley's column in " The Times " — He is a fine little fellow — as I think you know — but Barrie is able to make him feel like crying too often and he sees a good deal of Barrie and a good deal in him. I suppose *he* too is very remarkable.

But I agree with the writer in ' The Mask ' that Balfe and Barrie are twins — The English audience is almost always on the verge of breaking down without any keep — if a fiddle squeaks everyone's sniffing — if a leading actress trips over a carpet a big burst of emotion is waved up to her from 3000 hearts. And I for one think this rather a waste of time in a great nation. Otherwise Barrie is a duck. All sorts of stories are told of how kind he is with his money — giving right and left: and without letting folk know, you know. The sort of man Carnegie needed instead of which he had to put up with a private detective like Dr. R. S. Woodward whose whole idea seems to have been to discover cranks at all costs — Carnegie's cost — and then shake his head at them.

Very glad a new book is on its way — Don't get too successful, Nathan — these first books of yours have got to be beaten by you: since no one else in America seems trying to beat them. GORDON CRAIG

15. July. 1924.
RAPALLO.

Oct. 14, 1924.

My Dear Nathan:

It's awfully charming of you to be attempting to persuade Gest to invite me to America — i.e., Broadway — but what would poor Gest be able to find in me to boom — *I* have no Politics like Lady Diana; I have no Theories — like Reinhardt and Stanislawsky have — All I have is a bit of imagination and a genius for making other people rich —

Of course that is something to work on I admit and if Gest or anyone else knew how to *safeguard* all the little ideas as they were coming out of my head and how to transport them from my workshops to one American theatre, such a theatre might flourish for as long as the ideas were coming out —

As for showing off in a theatre for a season that is beyond me — I am not really up to that.

That requires a tough old showman who doesn't care a damn what he does so long as he excites the tails of the mob — he can do it brilliantly even in a sacred play. I am utterly incompetent for such a job — and regret it very much.

I have been practising swimming these last two weeks with regularity — for I thought that if perhaps I could swim the Atlantic, *that* would help poor Gest to a booming theme — but I broke down after the first 10 minutes in ocean —

The worst of the Theatrical Impressarios is that they all die so poor — Cochran has been ruining himself these last 10 years and in his Egoism believes it all due to not having been able (owing to a serious operation) to sign a contract with a man who swallows a duck whole and gets *into* a bottle. I could have told Cochran 15 to 20 years ago (i.e. after The Miracle) that to play the fool with Duse — Carpentier — Dolly Sisters — Moscow Art Theatre — Battling Siki — Rodeo — the Duck-swallower would render him a poor man. I could have shown him how to build up a great name for himself — keep his health and pocket a fortune and enjoy the last 15 years of life — And the fellow wouldn't have listened.

They have *pocco cervello,* these impressarios — and are weak of purpose, yet seem brilliant and powerful personalities — They cannot see ahead — or stay firm for six months — They are a disappointment and none of 'em has ever approached Barnum in daring

Yours

E. G. C.

The copy of your new book has not yet come — it is a success — I hope so.

THREE SCENARIOS

THREE SCENARIOS

Mencken and Nathan, after writing Heliogabalus, *considered the joint authorship of other plays. Of these I am privileged to present the scenarios of three, each of which fell through because one or the other of the men rejected the ideas before they were treated to elaboration. Two of the ideas originated with Mencken, one with Nathan. The Mencken pieces (the first of which appears as a Letter to Nathan) never went beyond the stage of short synopses; though they have a local habitation they never received a name. The Nathan scenario, however, attained to the dignity of an eleven-page synopsis, with hints of experimental dialogue, and with the name* Pleasantville. *I wonder whether it was not partly suggested by Ludwig Thoma's* Moral, *a version of which Mencken and Nathan once made under an assumed name. (This is not to be confused, however, with the adaptation of the play given during the season of 1925–26 in New York. Charles Recht and Sidney Howard are not, of course, pseudonyms).*

At any rate Pleasantville *in the rough form that I have before me, suggests also overtones of Hoyt's* A Temperance Town. *It is, in effect, a malicious dig at the virtuosi of virtue, in any town that carries its burden of self-conscious holier-than-thous.*

It is of passing interest to notice that, in the three out-lines here given, honors — or dishonors — are divided about equally between the sexes. The first of the Mencken scenarios lines the outraged males against the predatory females, with a rousing victory for the less deadly of the species. The second shows man in no new rôle — that of a willing slave to the external charms of womankind. It is in the Nathanian opus that we receive the psychological surprise. For, in Pleasantville *it is the men who are the virtuous dunderheads and the women who uphold — not vice, surely — but cheer and personal freedom. Nothing new here, either, from the biological standpoint, but it is none the less amusing to discover, in the scenario of a confirmed bachelor, that it is the ladies, married and single, who rise to the occasion.*

Pleasantville *might have made a good satiric farce, although one may discern even in the outline a certain boozy sentimentality. All the authorial sympathy is as plainly with license (in both the spirituous and spiritual senses) as is that of any melodramatist with his hero* sans peur et sans reproche. *Perhaps the whole thing originated, regarding it in the light of the " newer " psychology, in Nathan's sub-vocal remark. " How dry I am! " In any case, though we may not have missed an important play, nor an original one, we have undoubtedly missed one that would have sparkled with the spicy and epigrammatical quality of Messrs. Mencken and Nathan at their conversational best. The play would have had, too, a quality that is all too rare in American writing, past or present: malice, in both the English and the French senses.*

The second Mencken scenario holds the least promise. His first, however, might have produced an important piece, unless its frivolous element prevailed to the detriment of the serious issues involved. It should have been written.

I. G.

I

DEAR GEORGE: An idea for the new play entertains me. It is to make the central character a respectable but still intelligent married man of about 45, who has gradually succumbed to the advancing demands of his wife and daughter. They are not mere suffragettes. They are gals who have got a notion that women are badly treated — in brief, the martyr complex — and who constantly bawl about it and reach out for the reins. They regard him as a mere boob. The conflict comes when the daughter catches a beau and preparations are making for the wedding. Mother and daughter lay down the law to the candidate, attempting to make a slave of him. Then papa, suddenly aroused, goes to the rescue, and the battle joins. The point of it is that, on the test, papa turns out to be much more intelligent than his wife and daughter. In the big scene he tackles the former head on, describing their married life in cold blood, but with some wit — and especially the means whereby his wife snared him. Such a scene was in a short story by David Graham Phillips. We could do it much better. Act I: The Bolshevism of the mother and daughter. Act II: The revolt of papa. Act III: The gals, floored, come in and surrender. Give this your thought. Such a conflict, of course, is not new, but we could get a good deal of novelty in it.

H. L. M.

II

1st Act

The head steward's office aboard the Prinz Heinrich. The head steward and his assistant are behind their desks with the dining room chart before them. In front of them are passengers arranging their seats at table. Most of them are men but among them are a few old baggages wearing impossible veils and leading dogs, etc. Room stewards rush in and out with baggage. A tremendous crowd and confusion.

Two of the men drop out and converse down stage. " Did you see her ? " It develops that a cutie is aboard. The only one. All try to get seats at her table. They try to impress all sorts of yarns on the head steward. One claims to be an ambassador, another is a brother-in-law of the head of the line. A third is making his hundredth trip and demands favors. Finally one bribes the head steward with $25.00, another hearing of it raises him to $50. The steward then cooks up reasons for ousting No. 1, who raises a big squawk. Scarcely has he settled this when a third offers him a $100.00 and he proceeds to oust No. 2. The latter screams for the captain and threatens to sue the line for damages.

In the midst of the turmoil, the cutie walks in. She is a very young and pretty girl and her entrance causes an immediate hush. She drops her handbag and four or five men rush for it, rolling over one another on the floor. A Frenchman rushes up and speaks to her and he is promptly knocked down by an American. The cutie pretends that she is unaware of the cause of the excitement, but actually, of course, she knows what it is about and enjoys it very keenly. At the conclusion of the scene and of

215

the act, the whole crowd is put to flight by the entrance of the captain, who, on catching sight of the fair one, announces in a Hindenburgish manner that she will sit at his table. Exit the cutie. As the curtain falls, the whole crowd is rushing upon the captain in an effort to get invitations to join him and her.

2nd Act

The upper promenade deck of the ship. During this act, the rows between the various men are developed at length. The Americans fight with their fists and are rushed off to the hold in chains. The denouement that I have in mind is a duel between the first and second officers of the ship, with grotesque seconds. The cutie should be brought on at the climax of the act. Perhaps it might be managed by having her walk in and break up the duel.

3rd Act

The ship is now entering the Bay of Naples. All of the male passengers are bandaged. They have been wounded in the various frays of Act 2. The dénouement needs working out. My original scheme would probably cause the moralists to raid the play. Perhaps a better plan would be to have a great big overgrown ruffian of a boy rush in and address the cutie as mother. Another plan would be for it to appear that her fiancé has been aboard the ship all the while and that she has punished him for some late offense by refusing to speak to him. Then another would be for the men to throw dice for her and to arrange that the winner is to kidnap and marry her; then have her fiancé come in as the ship drops anchor — a gigantic creature, twice as large as any of the others.

216

III

PLEASANTVILLE

Rough Synopsis for a Comedy in Three Acts

ACT I

SCENE: The front porch and lawn of the house of Henry Silsbee, a leading citizen of the little town of Rome, in a middle Western State. It is eight-thirty of an evening in the early Spring and the leading citizens, their wives and some of the older boys and girls are here as Silsbee's guests to greet Morton Parker, the man who has gained state-wide celebrity for the success of his moral crusades in a dozen or more neighbouring towns. Parker has been invited to show Rome the light. Silsbee and his committee have extended the invitation. On this committee are several of the leading females of Rome, but not Mrs. Silsbee. The latter is an attractive, though plain, woman of say thirty-six. She is not especially against the invitation, nor is she in favor of it. She simply doesn't see the good of stirring up things: they might be worse — and let well enough alone. But Silsbee and the others prevail and now all is ready for the reception.

While waiting, the various characters enunciate the preface to the play. The little town, with the hills and river in the background and the cottages lighting up here and there as darkness falls, is peaceful, charming. One can hear the crickets and, now and then, the plaintive whistle of a train winding through the far valley. The children play merrily on the lawn; there are snatches of love conversation; several of the guests (not the Committee of Six) are nicely pickled; one hears a bit of harm-

217

less scandal relating to buggy-rides, hay-rides, lawn fêtes, and the like; the village sport rolls by in his Ford on his way to the night's performance of the No. 5 "Blossom Time" company at the local Opera House; a vagrant Italian is heard grinding out on his hurdy-gurdy the latest fox-trot. The atmosphere of happiness and contentment is established. Yet in the midst of this patent happiness and contentment, the Committee of Six is rehearsing the town's sins and lack of moral endeavour. So-and-So is up to this, it appears; and So-and-So is up to that. Gus Paulhauser is running a blind pig somewhere on the edge of the town and Silsbee's brother-in-law, Louis Tompkins, has been hitting up the red-eye and beating his wife. Immoral and seductive shows like the aforementioned "Blossom Time" have been given monthly in the Opera House; Mae Murray has been permitted in the Little Dream Movie Palace on Main Street without interference. Rome, in short, has been getting too loose — didn't Mary Callon, the seamstress' nineteen year old daughter, run away and marry an actor in a recent "Uncle Tom's Cabin" troupe and nothing has been heard of her since?

So be it.

And so enter Morton Parker!

Parker gives ear to the tale of Rome and shakes his head. Things, truly, are bad! He tells of his enterprises in the neighbouring towns, of the great good he has done. He will — God willing — do the same for Rome. The name Rome is a handicap. Rome was sinful, vicious. It shall be changed. A noble beginning. Suggestions are freely given. Why not Pleasantville? This is the only state without a Pleasantville. Pleasantville it is.

Parker now proceeds to outline the work to be done by each member of the Committee. Clandestine booze shall be killed; there shall be no spooning by the young men and women (he whispers what it leads to, with many examples from neighbouring towns); there shall be no more " Blossom Time " troupes, no more Mae Murray pictures; no more buggy-rides and hay-rides; and curfew shall ring at ten.

Mrs. Silsbee is not convinced. She makes bold quietly to inquire what good it will do to clamp down such a lid? She sticks up for the young lovers (we use one couple concretely); she sticks up for a bit of a souse now and then; she sticks up for " Blossom Time " and Mae. But, though she does this with a pleasant humour, it is of no avail. And as a starter, Pleasantville's first curfew is ordered rung on the bell of the First M. E. Church fifteen minutes hence. The young people protest; so do the souses; so do some of the women. But Parker has his way. A telegram announces to Parker that the last blind pig in Chapel Hill (*née* Winesburg) has been suppressed. Another, delivered simultaneously, that the last prostitute has been driven out of St. Mary's (erstwhile Paris). Ah, that Pleasantville (quondam Rome) may have as good fortune! The bell on the First M. E. Church rings. One of the souses, who has been asleep under a tree throughout the act, jumps up excitedly and asks what's burning.

" Rome," responds Parker, piously. " And out of its ashes there is rising (he waves his hand in the direction of the young folk sadly homeward-bound) — Pleasantville! "

CURTAIN

ACT II

The Effects of the Moral Wave

SCENE: Main Street.

TIME: Six weeks later.

The stage is set very deep. One sees a row of trees skirting off at left and right and, behind a brick sidewalk, the small town stores, the " Little Dream " movie theatre, the Opera House, etc. These are in the last groove; the trees are nearer the footlights; the sidewalk nearer still; and still nearer is the street itself. Two oil lamp-posts unlighted. It is about fifteen minutes of six and dusk is settling. As the curtain rises, the organ-grinder of Act I is toting across the street his hurdy-gurdy, grinding out " Nearer, My God, to Thee." The " Little Dream " is now boarded up, a To LET sign conspicuously on its door. The Opera House is covered with a cheese-cloth announcing that it is now the headquarters of Morton Parker and the State Anti-Vice Society. The drugstore window has a display of beauty preparations.

Enter the young lovers of Act I, bound for the soda-fountain in the drugstore. They pause at the door. A brief love scene. In the midst of this, one of the policemen installed in the town as a Parker aide bids them move along. No more public spooning. They exit into the store. The policeman's eyes light upon the display of beauty preparations. In the centre is a lithograph of a woman in décolleté. The cop glances from the picture to the doorway wherein the young couple were spooning. He nods his head, as if connecting the situations. The lithograph is suggestive. He will have it removed. He enters the drugstore. Presently, the druggist's hand is seen removing the lithograph.

As this is going on, the souse of Act I has entered with his wife. He is dead sober. In Act I, a pleasant fellow, he is now — with his booze taken from him — a sourball. Where he has made boozy love to his frau in Act I, he now swears at her. They are joined presently by the village sport of Act I. The latter presents a gloomy spectacle. He details his sad life during the long six weeks. He lights a cigarette, cagily glancing right and left to see whether a cop is about. He brings out that cigarettes are under Parker's ban. At the right of the stage, a young girl sneaks along. She signals the village sport. He moves to join her. She is Silsbee's daughter. Parker has warned Silsbee *père* of the danger of allowing young men to spoon in the front parlour and the sport has not been able to " call " on Myra. The latter thus has to arrange secret meetings with the boy. Simultaneously, the scenes at right and left proceed. As, one after the other, the scenes draw to their conclusions and the characters go off, enter Parker and Silsbee from their headquarters. They discuss the great change for the better in Pleasantville. (We make Parker not a crook, but a reformer who honestly believes that he is doing good.)

Mrs. Silsbee enters. She is looking for Myra. Couples go past squabbling. Husbands have nothing to do but sit at home all evening with their wives. Wives nothing but to sit at home all evening with their husbands. No movies; no plays; the *Cosmopolitan*, *Snappy Stories* and *Breezy Stories* have been banned from the news-stand. Parker and Silsbee rehearse what they have accomplished. Mrs. Silsbee points out the flaws in their system. They have, she says, made the town moral, but they have coincidently made it damned unhappy. She points to the case of the souse and his wife, of the sport (a decent fellow at heart) and Myra, of the danger to the young folks, etc., etc. Silsbee and his wife come to figurative blows. A challenge. The cop comes on and calls Parker aside. He whispers something. " Arrest them both! " orders Parker.

" Arrest who? " inquires Silsbee.

" Arthur Lawson," responds Parker.

" What's he done? "

" The officer will tell you."

The cop spouts the story. Lawson, the sport, has been caught spooning on the grass back of the courthouse with a girl.

" Who was the hussy? " asks Silsbee.

" She wouldn't give her name," says the cop.

" Well, you did right, officer," observes Silsbee. " This sort of thing has got to stop! We must protect the young."

Rushes on Myra, sobbing.

The cop makes for her — " That's the girl! "

The scene between Mrs. Silsbee and the girl on the one side and Parker plus Silsbee on the other.

" This dirty-minded nonsense has gone far enough! " from Mrs. Silsbee.

[The scene goes on crescendo.]

The organ-grinder, in the distance, is meanwhile grinding out " Onward, Christian Soldiers."

" Onward, hell! " shouts Mrs. Silsbee, her arms about her crying daughter. " I've had enough — we've *all* had enough — of this uplift garbage. Peter Bristed has been beating his poor wife ever since you took his drink away from him; Mrs. Ludlow has gone half crazy sitting at home with her Albert since you closed the ' Little Dream '; girls like my Myra have to sneak out and hide and God knows what with their young men since you wouldn't allow the young men to call on them in their own homes. Onward hell, I say! I'm going to clean up this town of cleaners-up if it takes ten years. I'm going to make it *happy* again. And here " — she grabs up a brick — " is my first move! "

She lets the brick fly through the window of Parker's headquarters.

CURTAIN

ACT III

The Turning of the Worm

SCENE: Same as Act I.

TIME: Early evening of a day a month later.

When the curtain rises, it appears that Mrs. Silsbee has called together her anti-morals committee for a final report on its work. This committee, composed of women who have seen the town go to the dogs under Parker's régime, enter one by one (we can get laughs out of the different types), are received by Mrs. Silsbee, and presently get down to business. Mrs. Paulhauser, wife of Gus Paulhauser, who operated the local blind pig, makes the report of her great progress. Mrs. Bernstein, wife of the " lessee and manager " of the Opera House; Mrs. Springbaum, wife of the " lessee and manager " of the Little Dream moving picture theatre; Mrs. Burns, wife of the landlord of " that woman " who lives near the railroad track — each makes a similar report. The bomb is ready. Mrs. Silsbee dispatches them to their various posts about the town.

As the last of the women disappears, Silsbee enters. He seeks to dissaude his wife from her campaign against him, against his friend Parker. She merely smiles. He feels, and correctly, that something is up; but he doesn't know what it is. Parker, Silsbee announces, is coming to supper. Again, his wife smiles — but says nothing. She goes into the house. The souse of Act I heaves upon the scene, again nicely plastered. Silsbee is dumbfounded. Where did he get the booze? The souse merely grins, and begins singing. Parker enters. Silsbee grabs him. Something is wrong, he tells him. He can feel it in the air.

224

He relates the reasons for his tremors. Parker says bosh — no need to worry — the town is cleaned up for good. They go into the house as Myra and Arthur come on arm in arm from behind the house. It develops that Mrs. Silsbee has persuaded Art' to call on Myra every evening in the old-fashioned parlour way. A brief love scene between the couple. At the conclusion, Art makes off telling Myra, to her surprise, that he'll be back for her shortly and will take her somewhere for a lot of fun. She asks where. " You'll see," Art throws over his shoulder. . . .

Mrs. Bernstein's little son Irving enters breathlessly and tells Myra he must see her mother at once. Mrs. Silsbee is summoned. Irving whispers something into her ear, lest Myra hear. While Irving is whispering, Molly, Mrs. Burns' young daughter, hurries on and tells Mrs. Silsbee that her mother says that everything is all right. Another souse (who has been nasty while sober in Act II) enters jovially, carrying a huge bouquet of flowers. He is on his way home to present them to his wife. ' A great li'l woman! How I belove her! " etc.

All exit, save Mrs. Silsbee, who is joined by Silsbee and Parker. The scene between Mrs. Silsbee on the one side and the men on the other, working up from the similar scene *à trois* in the preceding act. In this scene, however, it is the men who wax hot. Mrs. S. has the reins in her hands and knows it. But she deals out her cards suavely and pleasantly — and one by one. During the progress of the scene, Art and his Ford sail on. Art calls to Mrs. Silsbee and the latter hails Myra.

" Where's she going? " demands Silsbee père.

" To the movies," replies Mrs. Silsbee.

" Movies? *What* movies? "

" At the Little Dream."

" But the Little Dream's closed! "

" No it isn't, dear." Sweetly.

Silsbee can't quite make it out.

A pause. Then —

" Is Deacon Tutwiler showing that ' Life of Christ ' picture for the benefit of the Methodist Sunday School Fund *tonight?* "

" No, dear."

" Then — *what?* "

" The Fox Film Company is showing Betty Blythe in " The Queen of Sheba."

The scene proceeds crescendo. Two more souses stagger past along the highway, singing at the tops of their lungs. A messenger boy (aetat 50) brings messages to Parker announcing the backsliding of several nearby towns. Several women pass with their husbands on their way to see a road company play " The Second Mrs. Tanqueray " at the Opera House. A wagon laden with *Snappy Stories* rolls up the road.

Silsbee and Parker accuse Mrs. Silsbee flatly. She tells them amiably just what she has done. She assures Parker that he is an honest man, but a mush-head. More messages arrive for Parker, telling him that other nearby towns have changed their names back to the old ones. One by one, the women of the anti-morals committee come on. Some are accompanied by their husbands, others by their beaux. All are beaming. All are dressed up in their gayest Winchell Smith last act duds. In the distance, the organ-grinder is playing the latest shimmy dance. One of the husbands dances the shimmy with his wife (with whom he has quarreled bitterly in Act II). The red light in " that woman's " house shows suddenly down near the railroad track. The voices of the two souses are heard yodeling " We Won't Go Home Until Morning." One of the men whispers to Mrs. Silsbee.

" In the cellar, under the coal bin," she tells him.

With three or four willing assistants, he hustles after the booze.

Mrs. Silsbee announces that Pleasantville has, by majority vote, changed its name back to Rome.

" The town has gone to hell," says Parker, as he takes his hat and prepares to depart.

" Hell," observes Mrs. Paulhauser, wife of Gus Paulhauser, " Hell, Mr. Parker, iss th' German word for Light! "

CURTAIN

THE ETERNAL MYSTERY
A FIFTEEN MINUTE PLAY

THE ETERNAL MYSTERY

PLAY IN ONE ACT

BY

GEORGE JEAN NATHAN

PREFACE

This little play, after several weeks of rehearsals, was originally presented, in 1913, before a single audience in the Princess Theatre of New York. On the theory that it was sacrilegious, the managers of the theatre, by a vote of three to one, ordained its immediate suppression. After its suppression in New York, the play was presented by Mr. William Moore Patch in the Pitt Theatre of Pittsburgh, where it apparently injured the sensibilities of no one and where it enjoyed a prosperous engagement. Encouraged by this, Mr. Patch next produced the play in the Washington Theatre of Detroit where, once more after a single performance, he was compelled by the directors of the theatre to withdraw it. Here again was the contention of impiety raised. Mr. Patch, like Mr. William A. Brady in New York, promptly resigned from the management of the theatre after this action on the part of the landlords. Several weeks later, Miss Beulah Jay, directress of the Little Theatre of Philadelphia, produced the play on the stage of that playhouse, where it seemed, once again, to offend no person and where, indeed, its engagement was twice lengthened. . . . The play has, of course, been shown on the Continent without hindrance or ethical condemnation.

In view of the circumstances attending the production of the play in two large and doubtless representative American cities and, at least to the author, the unintelligible attitude toward its thesis there displayed, the author deems it expedient to permit no further public presentation in the United States — the city of Chicago, a rational and evenly balanced community, being alone excepted. In that city, the author is pleased to grant any person who likes the play permission to perform it without payment of royalties.

A few words on the little play's theme. To argue that it is sacrilegious in a writer for that writer to present, through the medium of his central personage, every one of the stereotyped and hackneyed objections to the Deity voiced by the unbelieving and then, *within twelve minutes'* time, to convert that skeptic central personage to faith and to belief, is to argue that every missionary sent to the black and tan heathen races is given to the practice of a like irreverence. Our theatre, however, is a bizarre institution. It sees nothing profane or blasphemous in presenting the Saviour as a sizzling spotlight (" Ben Hur ") or as the inventor of a death-dealing submarine boat (in the motion picture " Civilization ") or as an uncouth actor (" The Servant in the House "), yet it shrinks — particularly in its Mosaic managerial depart-

232

ments — from such reverent and gentle and very beautiful things as Brieux's " Faith " and Andreyev's " Savva." The obvious sacrilege of such impious theatrical tinsels as " The Terrible Meek " and " Marie-Odile " — exhibitions of gross and evil taste aimed directly at the box-office — it hearkens to with awe and in devout silence. It views a team of horses toting a papier-maché chariot over a treadmill or a baby-spotlight halo-ing a seduced ingénue or a number of stagehands mimicking the roars of hungry lions in a Wilson Barrett play as an exalting religious spectacle, while it the meanwhile is somewhat puzzled as how to conduct its feelings and attitudes toward such a presentation as Shaw's " Androcles." Religion, so far as the theatre is concerned, is much like a cigar. A cigar, however good, is not palatable when smoked in the brilliant sunlight. A religious theme, however sound, is distasteful when aired in the glare of the footlights. This, therefore, the author's sole excuse for printing for library lamp this little play. If its theme is held by the reader to be too big for the dramatic treatment accorded it by the author, the latter, a critic by profession, may offer only in personal apology and in extenuation of his shortcomings the words of Samuel Johnson in defense of a critic-friend who found himself in a somewhat similar embarrassing predicament, " You may abuse a tragedy, though you cannot write one. You may scold a carpenter who has made you a bad table, though you cannot make a table. But — it is not your trade to make tables."

G. J. N.

December, nineteen hundred fourteen.

THE ETERNAL MYSTERY

Characters

A DYING MAN

HIS WIFE

HIS LITTLE SON

A PHYSICIAN

SCENE — *A room in a house — almost any room, almost any house. This particular room happens to have a large French window at the left, and this lone window happens to be thrown open. It gives out onto what, were it visible, would be seen to be a broad and very low veranda. The window is hung with long curtains of a light summery fabric, maybe madras. Although the window is open, the curtains happen to be drawn, allowing the sunlight to filter into the room but dimly. The side walls (of pale yellow) are bare save for three small pictures of Robert G. Ingersoll, Thomas Paine and Marconi. On the wall at the back hang two large pictures supposed to look like Voltaire and Ernest Renan, while on the mantelpiece, on either side of a clock, are to be seen small busts of Darwin and Giordano Bruno. There are the usual number of chairs, and there is a door at the right, far up stage, leading into another room.*

At the left, some four feet or so this side of the window, stands a long, low writing table strewn with numerous books and pamphlets. Among these the close observer might note Bronson C. Keeler's " Short History of the Bible," Whiton's " Miracles," " The Origin of Species," Nietzsche's " Human All-Too-Human," a couple of the works of John E. Remsburg (particularly

234

the latter's survey of the Bible), something of Huxley, something of Kant, something of David Hartley, something of Schopenhauer, something of Harriet Martineau, something of Faustus Socinus, something of Diderot, David Hume, Joseph Priestley and of von Hartmann. There might be noted, too, several magazines of comparatively recent date containing accounts of the scientific and biological achievements of Dr. Alexis Carrel, Elie Metchnikoff and Dr. Loeb. On the table, with seeming incongruity, there happens to be a cathedral candelabrum of silver, a raised candle socket in the centre with three lower candle sockets on either side, evidently placed in the man's room by his wife. Another candelabrum like it is visible on the mantelpiece. In the two far corners of the room are large bookcases laden with medical text-books.

The atmosphere is the atmosphere that prevails in any room in any house of any family of average mental, moral, physical, financial and social decency, although hardly the so-called " realistic " atmosphere with which such a scene on the stage would be invested by overly vain producers who seek by the exercise of elaborate theatrical appurtenances to divert attention from the playwright to themselves.

At the rise of the curtain, THE DYING MAN, fully clothed, is seated in a large chair to one side of the table, away from the window, but somewhat up stage. This, of course, is contrary to theatrical tradition, which specifies that all dying men must always die in bed in their nightgowns or on the floor (if the play be a military play) or must be standing up and suffer fatal attacks of heart disease during receptions in the last act just as the District Attorney is about to confront them with the proofs and arrest them. The man in this case is at the point of death after a despairing battle with phthisis florida (galloping consumption) — a disease that hits with bare knuckles and that with fine crafti-

*ness permits a man his full mental powers until the very end so
that he may the more completely appreciate and enjoy his suffer-
ings. Across the table from the man stands* THE PHYSICIAN.
It is about five o'clock of a summer afternoon.

THE DYING MAN

(*with perfect calm and in what is very nearly a normal
voice, broken now and then by a racking cough*)
What's *your* idea?

THE PHYSICIAN

(*shifting the candelabrum a bit to one side that he may
the better see the man's face*)
What's yours? You're a physician yourself — you've spent
your years fighting this awful thing — you know it from first to
last, from the first little cough to the last hemorrhage.

THE DYING MAN

Oh, I know it's but a matter of hours. Have you told my
wife?

THE PHYSICIAN

(*nodding*)
She's in there —
(*indicating the room at the back*)
with her tears.

THE DYING MAN

My little boy — don't tell him. The end itself will be enough
for him. Where is he?

THE PHYSICIAN

(*nodding toward the open window*)
On the lawn.

THE DYING MAN

What is he doing — who's with him?

THE PHYSICIAN

Bobby, *my* boy, and he are playing with the toys and things you had sent up.

THE DYING MAN

Toys?

THE PHYSICIAN

Yes, he told Bobby yesterday you had ordered some toys for him. They were delivered a short while ago.

(*the sound of youngsters' laughter and shouts is heard through the window*)

Doesn't that sound like it?

THE DYING MAN

Toys — oh, yes. I remember now — the ones I had Ruth telephone for.

THE PHYSICIAN

(*looking at* THE DYING MAN *hard*)

It's terrible, Rayburn, to see a man like you go this way without being able to do anything to help him. Great God —

THE DYING MAN

(*cutting in*)

Great God? Great *fiddlesticks!* If people would turn their churches, their praying cabarets, into laboratories — and begin thinking and investigating instead of getting on their knees to a superstition, their hundreds of thousands of tubercular fellow human beings like myself might be spared. Save souls? Rat-logic, I say! Save *lives!*

237

THE PHYSICIAN

Quiet, Rayburn — don't excite yourself. I've heard you go through all that many times before. This is no time —

THE DYING MAN

No time! I suppose now that I am about to die, you think I'll retract — that I'll lose my mind and call on that something you call God to take me to him! Well, you're wrong. I never believed less in a God in all my life than I do now. God — a creation of ignorant, superstitious minds! If Kellar, the vaudeville magician, had lived in the savage age, a lot of believe-what-they-readers would be worshipping him today. I repeat: I never believed less in a God in all my life than I do now!

(the door has opened as THE DYING MAN *is speaking, and through it comes* HIS WIFE. *As she hears the last words, a moan leaves her lips)*

THE WIFE

(with a world of tears in her voice)
Oh, Jim — don't!

THE DYING MAN

(after a pause)
Come here, my dear; come to me. I want you near me. I want to speak to you.

THE PHYSICIAN

I'll step into the next room — the door will be open — I'll wait until you call me.
(he goes out)

238

THE DYING MAN

Ruth, sweetheart, you know it's very little time now until I'll have to go. I want you and our boy to —
(*the words falter*)

THE WIFE

Be happy?

THE DYING MAN

To be happy and —

THE WIFE

Then *believe*. Oh, Jim, *believe!* All our life together I've prayed to God you would, and now in the hour of our separation I pray to you as well.

THE DYING MAN

If I only could!

THE WIFE

It's so terrible to think of you going this way — defiantly — with eyes that *will not see!*

THE DYING MAN

Going? I go nowhere, dearest love. I end! I end as a withered plant ends, as a rotten apple — as all nature when its day is done. Belief in some God is nothing but a self-deluding hoax, a trick to make death easier.

THE WIFE

But if you should be wrong — if when life has gone you *should* see?

THE DYING MAN

Ha, you see! Your God, too, is Fear, like the God of all you believers. If there is a God, why isn't he powerful enough

239

to *make* me believe; why is his influence so puny that thinking men of all time have found in their minds ample strength to doubt him?

THE WIFE

Through the doubt of one man, the faith of a million is strengthened.

THE DYING MAN

Nonsense. Through the doubt of some one man each marvelous discovery, each great invention, has been born. In doubt lies progress. "The infidels of one age have often been the aureoled saints of the next."

(*again the laughter and shouts of the youngsters penetrate to the darkened room*)

THE WIFE

(*pleading*)
For our boy's sake, Jim!

THE DYING MAN

For his dear sake — no. Let him have lesson from me. Let him live his life fearlessly, honestly, and with faith only in himself — and in you — and in the woman he'll some day come to love. Let *that* be his religion. Don't let him trust blindly and ignorantly in something that doesn't, that *can't* exist.

THE WIFE

He shall learn from the Bible.

THE DYING MAN

(*with a weak laugh*)
The Bible! Then may Fate have pity on his little white heart! The Bible — an immoral fiction fake sanctioning po-

240

lygamy, slavery, massacre! Inspired by God? And it says the earth is flat; it says the earth is the centre of the universe; it says that a man should be vindictive, revengeful — " an eye for an eye, a tooth for a tooth "; it teaches that human sin can be transferred to an animal; it says that the blood of a bird killed over running water is medicine —

THE WIFE

(*breaking in*)
Old arguments — the Bible — it can't be taken literally, Jim!

THE DYING MAN

(*heedless*)
— its God-given commandments plagiarized by a thieving deity from the law codes of infidel India and Egypt; Genesis full of more futile paradox than Chesterton or any other clever smart-aleck; with Humbolt, Darwin and Haeckel showing to us that this God knew mighty little about nature or anything else. And with Abraham Lincoln and a thousand — ten thousand — others who've lived and died for humanity proving that the God who said, " I will send the tooth of beasts upon them with the poison of serpents of the dust," was a blood-licking, cruel, contemptible inferior!

THE WIFE

(*persistent; in her same tone*)
He shall learn from the Bible.

THE DYING MAN

The Bible! *Learn* from the Bible! If a man had faith, the Bible would kill it. Who can answer the clear head of Ingersoll and its reading of the absurd thing? Remember? " God created the world, the hosts of heaven, a man and a woman —

placed them in a garden. Then the serpent deceived them and they were cast out. God was thwarted. Then he tried again, and he went on for sixteen hundred years trying to civilize the people. The task was too great. The people grew worse, so the merciful God sent the flood and drowned all but Noah and his family. Then he started again and failed again, and at the Tower of Babel he dispersed and scattered the people. . . .

THE WIFE

(*with a bit of a sneer*)
Ingersoll! A theatre box-office lecturer!

THE DYING MAN

(*still unheeding*)
" Finding he couldn't succeed with all the people, he thought he'd try a few. Again he failed, and these recherché people of his were captured by the Egyptians and enslaved for four hundred years. He kept on, and he kept failing. The people hated him and preferred the slavery of Egypt to the freedom of God. Failure — more failure. He tried again — took them into Palestine and had them governed by judges. Failure. Then by kings. The kings were mostly idolaters. Prophets were tried — but the people grew worse and worse. And God kept on failing. No schools, no sciences, no arts, no commerce. Then God took upon himself flesh and was born of a woman and lived among the people he had been trying to civilize for several thousand years. And then these choice people, following the law that God had given them, charged this God-man — this Christ — with blasphemy; tried, convicted and killed him. God had failed again. What an administration! "

THE WIFE

Details — little details.   God *lives* — Christ *lives!*

THE DYING MAN

(*after a brief pause*)
I feel stronger.   Knowledge and fearlessness have given me
strength.

THE WIFE

(*frightened*)
God is playing with you.

THE DYING MAN

Nature, maybe — but nothing else.   The mind is stronger
than any body, stronger than any God.   When Christian Science
eventually recognizes this and gets rid of its churchy hocus-pocus
it'll sweep the enlightened world.

THE WIFE

(*in despair*)
This in the hour of death!

THE DYING MAN

If there were a merciful God, my Ruth, would he devise an
hour of death like this?   Would he shoot galloping consumption
into my body and keep me quivering on the rack?   Wouldn't
he spare me, or else — wouldn't he kill me quickly, doubter of
him that I am?

THE WIFE

Maybe, maybe it's His way of punishment.

243

THE DYING MAN

Then every year this same equitable God punishes hundreds of thousands of tubercular wretches who believe in him just as cruelly as he is punishing me. What mercy, what wisdom! What a miserable farce!

THE WIFE

Jim, it isn't you who's speaking — no matter what you have thought, you can't say such things — now.

THE DYING MAN

It *is* I who speaks! Or, at least, the true thought of others speaking through me. And to the last I'll affirm it. I go out forever to the tune of no churchman's professional tears. To leave you, sweetheart, and our boy — that aches, *that* makes me afraid. *That* makes me tremble. For I know we'll meet in no hereafter. I wish I could fool myself — but I can't. I go to death fighting, struggling, cursing — with wrath in every line of my face — for death's the end of everything.

THE WIFE

(*in a wild prayer*)
Oh, God — great, good, all-powerful God in Heaven — Christ — forgive him, for he knows not what he says!

THE DYING MAN

(*reaching out his hand to her*)
You make it even more awful for me.

244

THE WIFE

(*in a rising voice*)
Forgive him! Make him see! Forgive! *Make* him see!
(*there is a dead pause*)

THE DYING MAN

(*calmly, coolly*)
Well, *why doesn't he?*

THE WIFE

Doesn't He — what?

THE DYING MAN

(*gradually working himself up to a white heat*)
Make me see! Why doesn't he " save " me — as they say?
If he's so all-great, so all-good, so all-powerful — so all-power-
erful — why doesn't he send into this little head of mine the
Thought of him — *belief?* All belief in God rests upon a miracle, upon several miracles. " Can miracles be established except
by miracles? " Why can your God no longer prove his divinity
— why does he weaken, stutter, falter, shrink back as men begin
to think more clearly and sanely about his existence? Why
shouldn't it be as simple for an all-powerful God — for an all-
powerful Christ — to convince in 1913 as it was 1913 years
ago? I'll tell you why! Because there never was any convincing in the first place.

THE WIFE

(*in supplicating sob*)
Forgive, O dear God, forgive him!

THE DYING MAN

(*rushing on heedless of his wife's words*)
Miracles — bah! You point to the Bible. The Ascension.
Why didn't Matthew, who was supposed to be present, think it
worth recording? Why was the account of this greatest miracle
on which faith rests merely interpolated in Mark and Luke? If
Christ really ascended, why didn't John, who was supposed to see
the ascension, mention it? Why don't the gospels agree on this,
the greatest and basic miracle?

THE WIFE

(*her words running into* THE DYING MAN's *tirade*)
Your brain's gone wild! This isn't you, my Jim! This is
the sacrilege of a —

THE DYING MAN

(*his face flushed, his body racked by coughing*)
The fact is — and
(*pointing to books on the table*)
those documents go to prove it — that the Ascension of Christ
wasn't claimed by his disciples. If Christ rose, why didn't he
appear to his enemies? Why didn't he do so in the sight of his
persecutors, where it would have done some convincing. Other
miracles, too! Matthew talks of twenty-two. Mark nineteen
or so, Luke eighteen and John seven — curing blindness, walking on water, turning water into wine, raising the dead, being
carried to the top of the temple of the Devil. Who can believe
such bosh? I tell you they never could be, never were! Miracles? Imagination! Crazy gabble! Insanity! Insa —
(*a sudden shiver shakes his frame. He brings his hands
quickly to his mouth. His face wrinkles in a hideous fear.*

246

A jerky quiver and he falls back into the chair, limp. A moment of silence. Then — a scream from THE WIFE. *She starts for the door, distracted, wild.* THE PHYSICIAN *appears on the threshold. He brushes the woman away, rushes to the man's side and bends over him. The woman stands terrified, silent. The ticking of the clock on the mantelpiece becomes acutely audible*)

THE WIFE

(*finally, in a hushed wail*)
Dead?

THE PHYSICIAN

(*shaking his head*)
No. This usually comes as a signal — a collapse — a short recovery; then —

THE WIFE

Then?

THE PHYSICIAN

(*slowly*)
The end.

THE WIFE

(*losing control*)
Oh, God, God — I can't bear it! I can't — I can't — I can't! Not this way! Oh, Christ, come to me, come to him, come to us! You can't let him go this way! For our boy's sake, come to him — and show him — and take him, when he must go — take him to You!

(*during the woman's outburst,* THE PHYSICIAN *goes over to the window and throws back the curtains. The horizontal rays of the late afternoon sinking sun shoot into the room. Suddenly the woman's sobs are checked. Her words stop. She stands transfixed, immovable, her gaze fastened on the wall opposite the window*)

THE PHYSICIAN

(*stepping anxiously toward her*)
Mrs. Rayburn!

THE WIFE

(*her eyes riveted on the wall, her voice far off and strange*)
Look!
(THE PHYSICIAN'S *eyes follow hers. On the right wall is the shadow of a small cross*)

THE DYING MAN

(*regaining consciousness; in a mumbled tone*)
Life — life — I want to live.

THE WIFE

(*throwing herself at his feet and pointing to the wall*)
Jim — Jim — see — *proof* — a miracle!
(*slowly* THE DYING MAN'S *gaze fastens itself to the woman's arm, to her finger, to the wall, to the sign of the cross*)

THE WIFE

A miracle!

THE DYING MAN

(*slowly bringing his eyes away from the wall and gradually sweeping them in a semicircle around the room until they rest upon the table at his side*)

248

A miracle?

(*his eyes meet the candelabrum. With a weak hand, he gropes for it, reaches it and sends it crashing to the floor. As the candelabrum falls, the shadow of the cross on the wall* [*the reflection of the candelabrum*] *disappears*)

A miracle? A candlestick!

(*even as* THE DYING MAN's *words are on his lips, and even as the sign of the cross disappears from the wall with the toppling over of the candelabrum, the shadow of another cross — larger than the first — takes its place.* THE DYING MAN's *eyes set upon it.* HIS WIFE *with a wild cry sinks to the floor at his feet.* THE PHYSICIAN *makes to go to her*)

THE DYING MAN

(*half rising in his chair*)

A sign — a miracle — Christ, I believe!

(*the sign of the cross becomes larger, clearer*)

Forgive me! Forgive me!

(*the shadow of the cross becomes still larger, still clearer*)

I BELIEVE AT LAST!

(*he lifts himself up for a second and then — a pause — he falls back — dead. At this moment, a shout of laughter is heard in the direction of the veranda, and the man's* LITTLE SON *runs into the room through the broad low window holding aloft a large Japanese bird kite*)

HIS LITTLE SON

(*breathless*)

Oh, papa! Will you — will you come out and — and hold my kite for me till Bobby flies it? I ain't — big enough. I can't hold it up high.

(THE PHYSICIAN *goes to the child, puts his arm on the lad's shoulder and quietly takes the kite from his wondering hands. And as he does so, the sign of the cross, now twice as large as before — the reflection of the child's cross-shaped kite in the sharp sunlight — fades from the wall. A silent, hushed moment, and the curtain falls*)

Note to the producer:

At the rise of the curtain the candelabrum on the table is placed in such wise that were the sun to hit it the shadow of a cross would not be reflected. The physician, at his first speech, stands at the far side of the table, that is, toward the wall, and, while speaking to the dying man, casually changes the position of the candelabrum. This is made to seem fortuitous to the audience, the physician moving it as if to get a better look at the man opposite. It also accounts for the fact that the candelabrum has not hitherto cast the shadow.

LOVE: A SCIENTIFIC ANALYSIS

A Juvenile Burlesque, Protoplasmic
Ancestor of *the American Credo*,
Répétition Générale, Clinical Notes,
etcetera, etcetera, confected by
G. J. N. *aetat* sixteen.

SNAPSHOT DURING COLLEGE DAYS

LOVE

A Scientific Analysis

BY

GEORGE JEAN NATHAN

The author desires to acknowledge his indebtedness for the valuable statistical assistance given him by Dr. Rudolph C. Ferguson, of the New York State Hospital for the Insane.

I

Let us take a typical young man and young woman who are typically in it and, employing them as specimens in clinical research, essay for once and for all to get at the bottom of the blamed thing. Here, for example, on the right, we have Mr. Beauchamp Kraus; here, for example, on the left, Miss Bermuda Dampjofer — both presumably in their right minds and senses and yet deriving an unparalleled *ecstasis* from such inscrutable procedures as the treasuring, on the side *de* Kraus, of a pressed jonquil that erewhile embellished the Dampjofer middle, and on the side *de* Dampjofer, of a rhinestone dingus shaped like a pretzel that, erst clasped prominently upon the expansive Kraus Little Mary, thoughtlessly betrayed to the world the closely guarded secret that young Kraus was a member of the mysterious Greek order of the Jersey City Dental College known as the Egyptian Graveyard Spooks. What is this *emoção* — and why? What is it that causes the young M. Kraus each day to put at least ten cents' worth of vaseline on his hair, to go in for violet socks, to eschew the company of his quondam boon male camarados?

253

And what that causes the Mlle. Dampjofer to send the coupon and the fifteen cents in stamps for a liberal sample of the massage cream that will make her look exactly like Della Fox — that causes the Mlle. Dampjofer to roll a wistful pupil to the moon? The professor who can solve the mystery is the professor who knows where trombone players practise.

But let us not be baffled ere we start. Let us consider the possible reasons for the Kraus-Dampjofer *dignus vindice nodus* in logical sequence.

First then, is it reasonable that the M. Kraus is thus enchanted by the Mlle. Bermuda Dampjofer because the Mlle. Bermuda Dampjofer is — let us for argument admit it — a sightly wench? It is not. And why is it not? Because, pleasant to the Kraus eye though the person of the Dampjofer is, the M. Kraus would be the first to admit that the person of the Dampjofer was, even so, of a vastly less beautiful aspect — by the standards of beauty (Pg. *beldade*) pure and simple — than the perfect wax dummies one sees in the modistes' windows on the Avenue. But, ha ha, the Kraus exclaims, this is droll, absurdo: the Bermuda Dampjofer is a creature of flesh (As. *flaesc*) and blood (Ohg. *bluot*), the dummies mere wax [1] and sawdust [2] — there's the difference.

Again, therefore, let us consider. We now have the M. Kraus' confession that it is not the unmatchable beauty of the Bermuda Dampjofer that floors him, but the fact that the Bermuda Dampjofer, unlike the surpassingly beautiful wax models, is alive. The M. Kraus, we then take it, is in love with the Bermuda Dampjofer not primarily because he is beguiled by her looks (Pg. *beldade*), but because she is living organism (F. *organisme*). Here, of course, our investigation takes an obviously simple turn. The M. Kraus is certainly not enamoured of the

[1] Pol. *wosk*.   [2] Produced by the attrition of a cutting-tool.

254

Bermuda Dampjofer merely because she is alive, for were this true he would be enamoured not of the Bermuda Dampjofer alone, but of a thousand and one other equally alive young women — forsooth, with all living young women! Let us, accordingly, dismiss this *prämisse* as ridiculous, and pursue another tack.

If, as we have shown, the Kraus is actually not, as he would call it, " in love " (*imbecilis stupendis*) with the Bermuda Dampjofer because of the Bermuda Dampjofer's (*1*) unsurpassed beauty or (*2*) aliveness, is it not possible that he may be, as he would call it, " in love " [1] with the something above these, the something finer, the more noble, the more spiritual — to wit, the Bermuda Dampjofer soul (F. *Marguéry*). Possibly. Let us see.

While the soul is more or less an intangible article, it may be possible fairly to analyze and sum up this Dampjofer especial soul in terms of its appraisal — not untypical — by the M. Kraus. This Dampjofer especial soul consists, therefore, in the Kraus estimation, as in the estimation of every Kraus in love with every Dampjofer, of (*1*) a mysterious far-away look in the Dampjofer eyes, (*2*) a kind and affectionate disposition on the part of the Dampjofer, and (*3*), finally, a complete Dampjofer sympathy with the Kraus likes and dislikes. Let us, accordingly, analyze in turn each of these Dampjofer soul attributes.

First, the mysterious, far-away look in the Dampjofer eyes (*ocularia melancholia*). This mysterious, far-away look, far from being peculiar to the Dampjofer of the Kraus passion, is, as the Kraus at heart knows, in reality the identical look that one notices in the eyes of every dog, mutt or otherwise. Therefore, since the Kraus, even at the height of his amorous delusions, would probably not think of leading a dog to the marriage altar,

[1] See Professor Hugo Disback's " Essay on the Intelligence of the Dachshund," p. 812.

it must be clear to the Kraus that it is not this first of the Dampjofer soul attributes that intrigues him.

Let us therefore consider the second, *viz.*, the kind and affectionate disposition. If it were true that the Kraus was to be drawn into his present extraordinary condition of *Flora sendis*[1] by this second attribute alone — i.e., by a kind and affectionate disposition — two conclusions would be plain. *Primo*, that since it is readily to be granted that the Dampjofer has not a monopoly on the kind and affectionate dispositions in the world, the Kraus would succumb equally to any other kind and affectionate disposition. And *secundo*, that since a kind and affectionate disposition is not confined to human beings but is to be encountered also, and in great and very beautiful degree, among the lower animals — like the mysterious far-away look in the eyes, primarily in dogs — it would follow, as in the instance of the Dampjofer soul attribute A, that the Kraus would here again (were the layman's process of ratiocination to be trusted) be likely to fall in love no more deeply with the Dampjofer than with Bruno, his pet mange-entrepreneur.

We come, then, to the Dampjofer soul attribute C, *viz.*, the complete sympathy with the Kraus likes and dislikes (Am. *hokum*). This we may promptly dismiss with the observation that this attribute C, standing apart and alone, while it might conceivably bring a certain Kraus to marry a certain Dampjofer, would assuredly not of and by itself bring to a Kraus the melodious mood as of walking-on-air, the complete amorous enchantment, the present overwhelming *romanticismus*. And since our investigation is concerned with these latter excitements, grouped together under the term known as Love, we may dismiss the attribute C as immaterial and irrelevant.[2]

[1] So named by Dr. P. P. Gambrinus, of Tusculum College.

[2] See Prof. Dr. Alois Wabler, "Lectures on Epidemic Encephalitis With Stupor," Vol. IV, Lect. III, Pg. 124.

II

We turn now to the other Kraus-sensed virtues, customs and stratagems of the Dampjofer and to their possible relationship to the current Kraus ebullition.

First, the Dampjofer trick of running the Dampjofer fingers through the Kraus hair, a manœuvre highly agreeable to the Kraus.

Admitting that this manœuvre is productive of pleasure for the Kraus — but also remembering that it is essential that in our investigation we duly and properly separate the manœuvre from its *chauffeuse*, that we may determine exactly the reasons, if any, for the Kraus' condition — we must be brought to the conclusion that the Dampjofer manœuvre is precisely akin to the manœuvre enjoyed by the Kraus when Gus, the tonsorial professor, visits upon the Kraus head (Am. *coco*) the monthly shampoo. Obviously, therefore, since the Kraus would think of the Gus, the tonsorial professor, in terms no more personal than he would think of Bruno, the pet mange-entrepreneur, we must grant that the fingers-through-the-hair phenomenon has nothing to do with the Kraus efflorescence, and pass on to the next hypothesis.

The next hypothesis: the Dampjofer holding of hands.

Here, plainly enough, we have merely what the manicure girl does — has long done — to the Kraus when the Gus has finished with the Kraus head (Am. *bean*). And, a hand being merely a hand, and holding a hand being merely holding a hand,[1] the thing can obviously be no novelty to the Kraus. It therefore cannot be the Dampjofer's holding of hands that is responsible for the exceptional Kraus mania (*presenti Tiffani*).

[1] See Dr. Herman Rochambeau's "Sensatory Science," Chapter XXV, Pg. 409, Paragraph 14.

Terzo, the Dampjofer playing of the piano.

This cannot be responsible since, were piano playing the one thing which bestewed the Kraus, the Kraus would, if for no other reason than that it bestewed him the more satisfactorily, buy him a pianola and remain a bachelor.

Quarto, the intriguing empyreuma of the perfumes, sachets and talcums sprinkled upon the Dampjofer.

Again no. And why? For the simple reason that man is projected into amour always in proportion as, and in the degree that, the object of his ardour is unattainable. It would be manifestly absurd, therefore, to believe that the Kraus fell thus deeply in love with scents readily obtainable at from 25c to $1.00 the box and bottle at the nearest drugstore. We must so look elsewhere.

Quinto, the Bermuda Dampjofer conversation.

This conversation, typical of every Bermuda Dampjofer, may be set down approximately as follows:

1. I like the two-step better than the one-step (or vice versa).
2. I a-*dore* James K. Hackett.
3. Reading hurts my eyes.
4. You never noticed I had a new dress (or hat) on.
5. I de*test* windy weather.
6. Not at all; I *like* cigar smoke.
7. Maybe, but she looks awfully chorus-girlish.
8. I think you're *aw*-ful!
9. I just love babies. I'd give anything if I had one of my very own.
10. I don't see how a man can drink whiskey. Ugh!
11. There it goes again! I don't know what can be the matter with me. I'm for-*ever* dropping it.
12. Don't be ab-surd. But I am awfully fond of his mother. She's perfectly *char*-ming.

13. I don't know what it is, but I simply *can't* get up in the mornings.

14. I dislike him intensely. He's so *gross*.

15. I know she's not pretty, but she always looks so *smart*.

16. *Guess* who I saw this afternoon?

17. Men are so peculiar. Why, she's at least thirty.

Since this conversation is readily recognizable as common to the great majority of young women of the Bermuda Dampjofer *aetat* and culture, we must fail to grant that it can be this factor that produces cardiac systole and diastole in the M. Kraus bosom when the M. Kraus bosom is in the Bermuda Dampjofer presence.

Sesto, the intrinsic intelligence of the Bermuda Dampjofer.

The Bermuda Dampjofer, like nine out of every ten Bermuda Dampjofers, believes implicitly in the following philosophies and faiths:

1. That if the Bermuda Dampjofer nose itches, it is a sign that the Bermuda Dampjofer is either going to meet a stranger or kiss a fool.

2. That if the Bermuda Dampjofer right ear burns, it is a sign that someone is saying nice things about the Bermuda Dampjofer.

3. That if the Bermuda Dampjofer left ear burns, it is a sign someone is saying mean things about the Bermuda Dampjofer.

4. That if a piece of tea leaf is found floating around the top of the Bermuda Dampjofer tea-cup, it is a sign that the Bermuda Dampjofer will be married before the end of the year.

5. That if the Bermuda Dampjofer accidentally puts on her lingerie wrong side out, it is still another sign that the Bermuda Dampjofer will be married before the end of the year.

6. That if the Bermuda Dampjofer takes the last macaroon

off the platter, it is a sign that the Bermuda Dampjofer will be an old maid.

7. That if, after one lusty blow, the Bermuda Dampjofer's birthday cake reveals five candles still burning, it is a sign that it will be five years before the Bermuda Dampjofer gets married.

8. That if the Bermuda Dampjofer gives a young man of her acquaintance a pen knife as a gift, the Bermuda Dampjofer and the young man will inevitably quarrel unless the young man exercises the precaution to give the Bermuda Dampjofer a penny.

9. That if, while promenading, the Bermuda Dampjofer and her escort walk on either side of a water hydrant or other obstruction instead of both walking 'round it on the same side, it is a sign that they will have a misunderstanding before the month is over.

10. That if the Bermuda Dampjofer can hold a lighted match in her fingers until it becomes completely burned up, it is a sign that the Bermuda Dampjofer's young man really loves her.

Since, as in the case of the Dampjofer repartees above considered, these philosophies and faiths — as will also be readily agreed — are common to the great majority of young maidens, we must similarly fail to grant that it can be this that brings the M. Kraus to lay a sedulous daily scrutiny to the creases in his pants and to the meticulous insertion of the scarf pin into the same hole it made in the cravat the day previous.

Thus are we brought to the conclusion — proved and established — that, since the M. Kraus cannot conceivably be in love with the Bermuda Dampjofer for the Bermuda Dampjofer's (*1*) looks, (*2*) actual existence, (*3*) soul, (*4*) manners, (*5*) little tricks, (*6*) talents, (*7*) agreeableness of presence, (*8*) conversation, and (*9*) beliefs, the only possible remaining reason for the M. Kraus being in love with the Bermuda Dampjofer is what may be described, in the phrase of Professor Pierre Flaherty of

Vassar College, as the Bermuda Dampjofer general personal charm. This so-called general personal charm, while superficially as vague as the Bermuda Dampjofer soul, may yet be analyzed at once as fairly and as searchingly as the latter. Let us proceed.

Careful study resolves this Bermuda Dampjofer general personal charm into the following principal component elements:

A. Clean, even, white teeth.

(Note to A: If the M. Kraus were to be fetched primarily by clean, even white teeth, the M. Kraus would obviously be more perfectly fetched by a flawless set of false teeth than the somewhat less perfect natural set vouchsafed him in the Dampjofer orifice.)

B. A trim figure.

(Note to B: See reference to the perfect wax dummies as opposed to infinitely less perfect Dampjofers.)

C. Attractive clothes.

(Note to C: See note to B.)

D. Gracious manner.

(Note to D: See references to the Dampjofer soul attributes B and C.)

E. A pleasant speaking voice.

(Note to E: If the M. Kraus were primarily to be fetched by a pleasant speaking voice, he would be fetched more decidedly by the professionally pleasant voice of a telephone Central operator — which he has heard several times every day of his life and long before meeting the Bermuda Dampjofer — than by the amateurishly pleasant voice of the Bermuda Dampjofer.)

III

Thus, finally, since we have proved that it is plainly impossible for the M. Kraus to be actually in love with any one of the many things concerned with the Bermuda Dampjofer, so by this same proof is it mathematically impossible for the M. Kraus to be in love with these things grouped together, that is to say, with the entity named Bermuda Dampjofer. That the M. Kraus is actually in love with the entity named Bermuda Dampjofer does not contradict this proof any more than the fact that one pea when rolled under the crossed fore and second fingers feels like two peas contradicts the essential fact that there's only one pea there after all. . . . And what is proved here of the M. Kraus may be proved with equal clarity, and in the same manner, of the Mlle. Dampjofer.

Therefore, obviously, there is no such thing as love.

BIBLIOGRAPHY

Europe after 8:15, with Mencken and Wright. John Lane Co., N. Y., Bodley Head, London. 1914.

Another Book on the Theatre. B. W. Huebsch, N. Y. 1915.

Mr. George Jean Nathan Presents. Alfred A. Knopf, N. Y. 1917.

Bottoms Up. Philip Goodman, N. Y. 1917.

The Popular Theatre. Alfred A. Knopf, N. Y. 1918.

A Book Without a Title. Philip Goodman, N. Y. 1919 (taken over by Knopf, 1920).

Comedians All. Alfred A. Knopf, N. Y. 1919.

The American Credo, with Mencken. Alfred A. Knopf, N. Y. 1920. (Revised edition, 1921).

Heliogabalus, with Mencken, Alfred A. Knopf, N. Y. 1920. (German-Theatralia-Verlag, 1922.)

The Theatre, the Drama, the Girls. Alfred A. Knopf, N. Y. 1921.

The Critic and the Drama. Alfred A. Knopf, N. Y. 1922. Bodley Head, London. 1923.

The World in Falseface. Alfred A. Knopf, N. Y. 1923. Bodley Head, London. 1923.

Materia Critica. Alfred A. Knopf, N. Y. 1924.

The Autobiography of an Attitude. Alfred A. Knopf. New York and London. 1925.

The House of Satan. Alfred A. Knopf. New York and London. 1926.

INDEX

265